WINE TASTING COMPANION

Wine Smart in a Day!

Napa & Sonoma Edition

Andy Hyman
with Marla Rosner

SNOB FREE PRESS
SAN RAFAEL, CALIFORNIA

Snob Free Wine Tasting Companion
Wine Smart in a Day
Napa & Sonoma Edition

Published by Snob Free Press
www.snobfreewinetasting.com

Copyright © 2015

Design and Production by Lynda Banks Design

ISBN: 978-0-9862443-1-5

Printed in China

SNOB FREE PRESS
San Rafael, California

Contents

Acknowledgments

The opportunity to write this book came from Don Rickard, who founded Platypus Tours, a truly wonderful organization that inspires many to connect with great wine experiences. Your feedback and encouragement for this book project was fundamentally inspirational.

A special shout-out to my loving wife, Marla Rosner. Without her writing and editing skills as well as her patience and tenacity, this book would not have come to fruition.

My friend Darren Whitcher validated the information and made important contributions to this book. As a chef with a background in food science and wine, he is not only a sought-after wine educator but has also been an invaluable resource to me on this project. His skill in making boutique wine tasting experiences the best in Napa Valley have inspired thousands of wine lovers; I could not ask for a more savvy advisor.

Many others have supported this effort:

- My sister, Leslie Lowe, who gave me thoughtful and prolific first-draft feedback. Your devotion to the task and to our relationship is deeply appreciated.

- Patricia Ravitz, who provided support and motivation through this whole process. She read the manuscript with great interest while providing excellent feedback as a novice wine taster.

- Karl Christensen, a fellow tour guide, consummate professional, and joy to be around, has taught me so much while sharing his knowledge and experience of Napa Valley.

- Alison Cohen, my daughter, who provided the critical perspective of a millennial in her feedback.
- Dena Positeri, our longtime friend, who spent much time reading the manuscript and offered encouraging and valuable comments.
- Lisa Sparacino, always a wise sounding board, gave me important and honest feedback as a wine novice.
- Kevin Mergardt, who is a daily mentor of fine wine tasting experiences. Your high standards for exceptional wine tasting experiences spurred me on my quest for knowledge about wine.
- Larry Robledo, of Robledo Family Winery in Sonoma, whose family story is incredibly inspiring. Thank you for cheering me on.
- Annette McDonnell of Paradise Ridge Winery. Your inspiration about wine and support for this book project was invaluable. The wine tasting experience in Kenwood is among the best in Sonoma because of you.
- Thousands of guests on my wine tours, who have provided an open heart and a thirst for knowledge about wine tasting in Napa and Sonoma in particular, and the wine making process in general.

Snob Free Wine Tasting Companion

1   Introduction

You may ask, "Why would we possibly need another book about wine?" This book evolved from my own pressing need to get up to speed quickly about wine after I was hired as a tour guide in the wine country in California's Napa and Sonoma counties. (Lucky me!) Before that, I had only a casual knowledge of wine, just enough to know a handful of famous wineries' names and to bring an average bottle of wine to a friend's house for dinner.

Imagine going from that point to leading tours of boutique and family-owned wineries, where I fielded innumerable questions from tour guests! Let's just say I was highly motivated to gather as much information as I could, and fast — just as you may be, to prepare for your wine country excursion. Also, I discovered that I very much enjoyed sharing what I was learning about wine with my guests.

esoteric [es-uh-ter-ik] — adjective
understood by or meant for only the select few who have special knowledge or interest [www.Dictionary.com]

The esoteric nature of wine became obvious to me. When I did my deep dive into the world of wine, I encountered words and phrases I associated with wine-snobs: words like "tannins," "long on the finish," and "bouquets." I decided to organize facts and information in a pamphlet and circulated it to my tour guests each day, believing I could enhance their experience by translating wine speak into language they could understand. And in fact, it worked! Every day, I heard people referring to my pamphlet. They even took it home as a memento of their trip.

I have led hundreds of tours and accompanied thousands of people in their wine tasting adventures in wineries in California's Napa and Sonoma counties. I've observed that when novice wine tasters learn the basics about wine and the process by which the wine gets to their glass, the esoteric language — which might sound snobby — doesn't intimidate them; they have more fun on their winery visits. A little knowledge makes them more confident about wine tasting and about purchasing wine.

Thus began my commitment to authorship. That pamphlet has grown into this quick and, hopefully, enjoyable read. Refer to it before, during, and after your trip to wineries. There are even note-taking pages to recall wines you enjoy, since one's memory can be challenged after the first few pours!

Quick Tips about Planning Your Winery Visits

I've always been a planner, but I know some people prefer the spontaneous, run-out-the-door-and-drive-to-the-wine-country approach. While it's hard to have a bad day in wine country, I strongly recommend asking yourself a few questions to help make it a really great day:

How much time do you have, and how many wineries do you hope to go to in one day?

Plan to visit wineries that are close together geographically if you want to squeeze in more than two or three. Choosing wineries that are far apart means you'll spend more of your day driving instead of wine tasting.

Is your main interest tasting wine?

Or, seeing wine caves and getting tastes from a barrel? Does getting a full tour of winery production facilities intrigue you? How about buying cool stuff in a winery gift shop? Eating lunch at picnic tables near the vineyard? Grassy areas for kids to play?

On the Internet, check out which wineries will meet your needs. Well-known name-brand wineries are often large and may be more heavily trafficked; small, less-well-known boutique wineries may be more serene and allow for a personal conversation with winery staff, or possibly even the wine maker.

How much do you want to spend on wine tasting?

Research the cost of wine tasting at various wineries. Tasting fees vary widely.

A Designated Driver

A point I feel compelled to address is a dilemma that most weekend wine tasters face: how do I imbibe, then later drive without putting my life (and the lives of others) in danger? If you are not paying for a driver or tour, it's no different than going to a party knowing you're going to drink and then drive home.

One person in your group should be the designated driver. Plan ahead, and stick to your plan. Generally, wineries are located a long way from populated areas, so if you aren't staying overnight in the wine country, you will likely have a long drive home.

"Bummer!" you say. "We all want to taste the wine." Here's the good news: the designated driver still gets to taste wine…a little. Though many people travel to wineries to enjoy a day of tipsy fun, in fact the wineries want you to taste small amounts of multiple wines. Your designated driver should taste just one tiny sip and pour out the rest of the wine in the glass into the "dump buckets."

The designated driver in your group must use discipline not to get inebriated from too much tasting. For some people that may mean one sip, and for others, no sips at all. Also: eat cheese and crackers, a sandwich or other snacks, and drink plenty of water over the course of your wine tasting day to slow the absorption of the alcohol in your system.

2   Navigating Your Winery Visit

Indulge your curiosity!

Don't be intimidated by the professionals who work in the wineries. They are experts and may use esoteric terms that aren't part of everyday language. Ask for clarification of words you don't know. Remember, the chief objective of wineries is to make great wine and sell it to you. As a prospective buyer, you are entitled to ask for "translations" of "wine speak" or anything else you would like to know. There are no silly questions. The more you learn, the better you will be able to hold your own with insiders and wine professionals.

Here are some ways to make your winery visits memorable:

* Find out about the person pouring your wine. Did you luck out and get the wine maker? This can easily happen if you visit small wineries. Or you may discover that the person pouring your tastes grew up in the area and knows everything about the history of the winery and the wine making process, from vineyard to bottling.

* If the winery is not crowded, ask for a small tour of the winery or barrel room.

* Ask specific questions about the history of the winery, if this interests you. How long has this winery been making wine? When were the first vines planted?

* Learn where the grapes were grown. Some wineries grow their own grapes right outside the tasting room; others make their wine from grapes they buy from growers.

- Let the person pouring the wine know the types of wine you enjoy, e.g., dry wines, sweet wines, "oaky," "crisp," "big bold reds." If you're not sure how to describe the flavor of a wine you just enjoyed, ask for the descriptions usually applied to that wine. Most wineries have wine tasting notes written by a professional wine taster that describe particular flavors in each wine.

- When you taste many wines, it can be hard to remember which ones were your favorites that you would like to buy. Take written notes after each pour about what you see, smell, and taste. Pages at the back of this book are designed for your wine tasting notes.

- Increase your vocabulary about wine tasting descriptors and the aromas, subtleties, and complexities of tastes. *(See Wine Aroma Wheel on pages 22-23 and the inside front cover.)*

- Did you know that your taste is strongly influenced by smell? If you take time to contemplate the aroma of wine, this will enhance your wine tasting experience. *(See Wine Aroma Wheel on pages 22-23 and the inside front cover.)*

- As you sip, swirl the wine around your mouth and over your tongue to get its full sensation.

- After you have finished a "flight" (a series of wine pours), you may "revisit" any varietal you particularly liked or are considering purchasing. This is a common practice. Just ask the person pouring the wine, "May I 'revisit' that (varietal name) one more time?" This is not an imposition; rather, it is considered a routine request by winery visitors.

Words to Know before You Start

Though you'll find a glossary at the back of this book, there are a few terms you will benefit from knowing as you start your wine tasting experience. The wine industry is full of wine speak that the average consumer doesn't know. These terms will help you understand the wine production process and how wine gets to your glass. Wine tasters often find that knowing the story about the wine they are tasting makes for a richer, more pleasant and more personalized tasting experience. Have fun!

Acidity: All fruits have natural acidity, the components in wine that make for a tactile sensation or feeling of a watery mouth. Fruits such as lemons, grapefruits and green apples have high acid content. When grapes ripen, acidity drops and sweetness increases. Too much acidity will taste "harsh" or "sharp," while a wine deficient in acidity will taste "dull" or "flat."

Balance: One of the most talked-about descriptors in wine tasting. A wine is balanced when it provides harmonious flavor. Balanced wines tend to be refreshing and pleasant to drink, with no one component awkwardly standing out. The key areas of balance include alcohol, acidity, tannin, sweetness, fruit flavor and minerality.

Brix Scale: The Brix scale is a measure of the percent of naturally occurring sugar, by weight, in unfermented juice. This is measured with a device called a refractometer or hydrometer in the chemistry lab to "back up" the results of the refractometer in the field.

Estate: A term used to indicate wine produced from grapes grown on winery-owned or leased land. This means the winery had control of the wine-making process from grape growing through finished bottling.

Fermentation: The process through which grape juice sugar is converted into alcohol.

Free-Run Juice: Free-run juice is the liquid produced by the natural breakdown of the grape cell wall from the weight of the grape berries as they are loaded into the press. About 60-70% of the available liquid within the grape berry, the "free-run juice," will be released by this process and does not require the actual use of a wine press. It is considered to be the highest quality juice for wine making.

Fruit Forward: A fruit forward wine's "bouquet" tends to emphasize scents like cherry or raspberry, as opposed to leather, vanilla, or mushrooms. A fruit forward wine emphasizes the characteristics that come from the grapes rather than from the wine making process, or perhaps extended aging in the maturation process possibly influenced by oak barrels or concrete tank aging.

Full-Bodied Wine: The sensation that the wine is heavy in your mouth. It is the sum of the effects of fruit, tannin and alcohol.

"Long on the Finish": The finish of a wine is the length of time the taste lingers in your mouth. "Long on the finish" means the taste lingers in your mouth for a period of time after you have swallowed the wine. Ideally, the taste will be "balanced," all the components of alcohol strength, acidity, residual sugar, and tannins will complement each other, and no single component will dominate.

Maceration: Maceration describes the process in which the grape skins are soaked in the juice from the grape (the "must"), causing phenolic materials (tannins, color and flavor) in the grape skins and seeds to be leached into the "must."

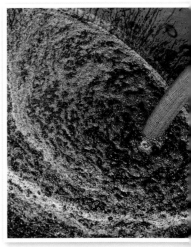

During this process, carbon dioxide is released, pushing the grape skins to the top, creating a "cap." The "cap" is then "punched down" (the juice is pumped over the cap) to create continued contact between skins and juice.

Malolactic Fermentation: A secondary fermentation process, naturally occurring or induced. A beneficial bacteria converts malic acid (very tart) in wine to lactic acid in order to produce a softer flavor. This adds a creamy mouth-feel and complexity to wines such as Chardonnay, and softens red wines such as Merlot and Cabernet Sauvignon. This process is spontaneous and natural in red wines, but must be forced in white wines.

Must: Must means "young wine." This is freshly pressed grape juice that contains the skins and seeds of the fruit. Making the must is the first step in wine making.

Reserve: Wine makers traditionally "reserve" grapes or wine from their best tasting barrels. They may also age the wine longer than other wines from the same vineyard. In some countries, use of the term "reserve" is strictly regulated, but in the U.S. it is a marketing term, with no formal or legal restrictions.

Tannins: Tannins are a "textural" element of wine that create a dry sensation in the mouth. They are a naturally occurring polyphenol (an organic compound) typically found in plants, seeds, bark, wood, leaves and fruit skins. As a typical component of wine, tannins add bitterness, astringency and complexity to the wine, and are mostly found in red wines, from the seeds and stems. Some white wines have tannins after being aged in oak barrels. Tannins are analogous to hops in beer, providing a texture as well as a feeling of dryness.

Terroir: (/ter' wär) A French word with no translation. This can best be described as the combination of soil type, slope, weather, microclimate, sun's orientation, humidity, and elevation of a vineyard. Terroir plays a big role in the quality of the grapes produced in a region.

Napa Valley in the autumn. Napa Valley's unique *terroir* is a factor in the award-winning wines produced here.

3   Types of Wine

Thistle is where a novice can begin to feel that snobs abound whenever the discussion of wine comes up. Basically, there are three types of wine: table wine, sparkling wine and fortified wine. Table wines, described as red, white or rosé, ferment naturally and make up the majority of the wine produced around the world. There are thousands of varieties of grapes; each variety produces a wine bearing its name, or, a "varietal."

Varietals

In the United States, a wine varietal is labeled according to the predominant grape types in the bottle. Examples of varietal types are: Chardonnay, Cabernet Sauvignon and Merlot. A wine varietal in the United States must be comprised of at least 75% of the grape type stated on the label. By contrast, in Europe wines are normally not named after the grape type, but rather after the region in which the grape was grown, e.g., Burgundy, Champagne, Bordeaux.

Sparkling and Fortified Wines

Sparkling and fortified wines have added carbonation and extra alcohol, respectively. Port and Sherry, which have higher levels of alcohol than regular table wines, are examples of fortified wines.

Note: In the United States, regulations prohibit the use of the term "Champagne." Only the Champagne region in France can use that term on labels. In the U.S., we refer to bubbly wine as "sparkling wine."

Based on a wine trade agreement between the European Union and the United States, the words "American Champagne," or "California

Champagne," could be used by those wineries making Champagne before 2006.

Napa, Sonoma, and Paso Robles in California, Walla Walla in Washington, and the Willamette Valley in Oregon do not permit the term "Champagne" on any bottles coming from their region, even if a winery there was grandfathered in under the national law.

4 Wine Tasting: The Basics

Though you may already enjoy sipping wine, you can refine and indulge your senses by seeing, swirling, smelling, sipping and savoring — the "Five S's".

See

Holding a glass of wine **in front of a white background is the best way to view the color of wine**. With a small amount of wine, slightly tilt the glass to view the wine color.

Why is color important?

You will see a range of colors depending on whether you are viewing white or red wine.

White wines will **gain** color as they age; red wines will **lose** color.

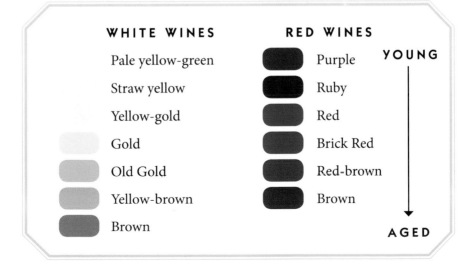

WHITE WINES	RED WINES	
Pale yellow-green	Purple	YOUNG
Straw yellow	Ruby	
Yellow-gold	Red	
Gold	Brick Red	
Old Gold	Red-brown	
Yellow-brown	Brown	
Brown		AGED

Individual perception can make a difference in how you identify color. Don't be surprised if a wine you would describe as "gold" is referred to as "straw yellow" by a wine server. The important thing to know is that wine color has no bearing on quality. It simply helps you anticipate what flavors you are likely to smell and taste.

"Rim color" is a way of guessing the age of a wine by observing its "rim" or "meniscus." By tilting the glass in front of a white background you can view the edge of the wine. A purple tint to the wine's edge can indicate youth, while orange-to-brown may indicate maturity. The wider the rim of water, the older the wine, due to the sedimentation of pigment molecules.

A wine may appear more or less saturated with color for several reasons:

- It may be older.
- Various grape varietals exhibit different colors.
- As white wines age in oak, they get darker through oxidation.
- Some wineries prefer unfiltered wine, which may show changed color over time.

Perception and taste

What we perceive just before we eat sets up our anticipation of what we will taste and affects our perception of flavors. Similarly, your perception of wine color will set up the "bouquet" you smell, and the flavor you are about to taste! Ask yourself: "Do I see colors of citrus, tropical fruits, tree fruits, floral, spices, red berries?" This is an important step in wine tasting. As plant-eating humans, odors in our diet trigger memories of aromas and flavors. This color association is a wine enthusiast's shortcut to understanding wines via color.

Swirl

Why swirl wine in the glass?

There is a practical snob free reason to swirl. The more oxygen that mixes with the wine, the more organic compounds that are components of the wine's fragrance will be released. Swirling will expose more air to the wine and release its "bouquet."

What is the best way to swirl?

Though you are not likely to see this anywhere but in wineries, it's really the gold standard in swirling methods. With only a small amount of wine in the glass, lay the glass on its side on a stable surface. Roll the glass back and forth about six inches. This will expose more wine to the surface of the glass than any other method of swirling and will add the equivalent of five years of aging to the taste of the wine. Then go directly to the "smell" phase.

About those wine "legs"

After you have swirled your wine, you may notice "legs" on the inside of the glass. There is a popular misconception that the legs revealed in swirling bear a relationship to wine quality. Should you hear such "information," feel free to ignore it. Though they add a visual perk to the aesthetics of wine tasting, legs have no bearing on the taste or quality of the wine. The width of the legs reveals viscosity. The number of legs reveals alcohol content, along with the rate at which the legs form.

High alcohol content produces more obvious "legs." Wines containing above 12% alcohol prominently show this Gibbs-Maragoni effect, named after the scientists who explained it.

Smell

You may already know that smell significantly affects our perception of taste. In fact, 80% of taste is created by smell. So to truly enjoy the subtle tastes of wine, your nose simply must get involved. Over 200 scents can be smelled in wine! But many people don't take enough time on this wine tasting step. Smelling in wine tasting is important because it helps you identify specific characteristics in the wine. Just as with tasting food, your experience of smell sets up your perception of taste after your visual inspection of the wine.

Once you have viewed the color and swirled the wine to release the bouquet, **take the time to smell the wine three times**. The third whiff will be different from the first and second, and will give you more information. Ask yourself: **"What kind of 'nose' does the wine have?"** "Nose" is a word often used to refer to the bouquet and aroma of wine.

Take a few seconds to identify what you are smelling!

Are you smelling citrus, tree fruits, tropical fruits, red berries, or black cherries; or perhaps floral bouquets, vegetal smells, such as fresh herbs or vegetables, or maybe spices, nuts or woods? Don't be disappointed if you don't associate the bouquet with any familiar smell. It can take quite a bit of wine tasting to become this discerning. Consult the Wine Aroma Wheel on pages 22-23 and the inside front cover for all the possibilities.

One of the best ways to wine taste is to practice smelling and identifying the wine bouquet. You may even begin to memorize the smell of different grape varietals. Start with Chardonnay and Pinot Noir and move to more complex varietals.

Bad smells in wine

In the course of tasting wine, you may also learn to recognize some less-than-enjoyable smells that indicate the wine is defective or "faulted." These smells are likely to be found in wines stored at home, or left open too long and served by the glass at restaurants. At a restaurant, don't feel compelled to accept a wine that smells bad.

If you discover a bottle of wine with any of these odors, it's time to toss it out!

SMELL	WHY?
Vinegar	Too much acetic acid in wine
Sherry	Oxidation
Cork (wet-cellar, musty)	Wine absorbs taste of defective cork
Sulfur	Too much sulfur dioxide*

*Sulfur dioxide is used in wine making to kill bacteria, prevent unwanted fermentation, and as a preservative. If overused, sulfur dioxide can cause a burning sensation in the nose.

The Wine Aroma Wheel and how to use it

The purpose of the Wine Aroma Wheel (on next pages and inside front cover) is to facilitate communication about wine flavor by providing a standard terminology.

1 Start in the center of the wheel where there are very general terms.

2 Move to more specific terms in the outer tier.

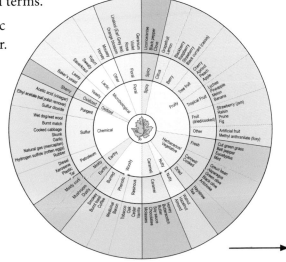

The Wine Aroma Wheel

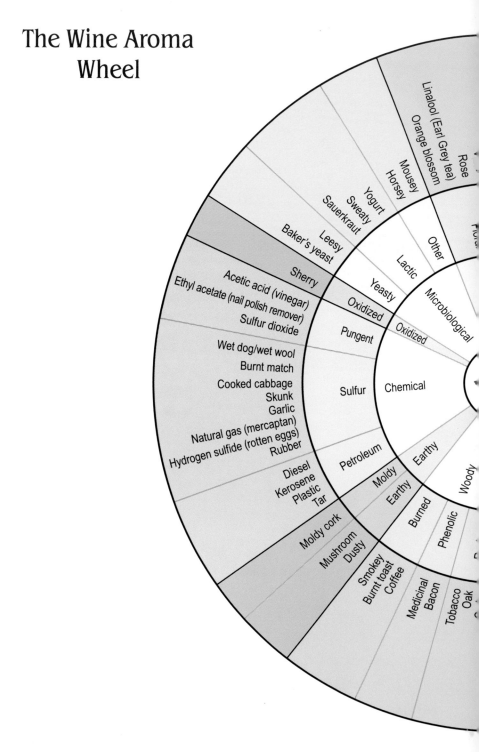

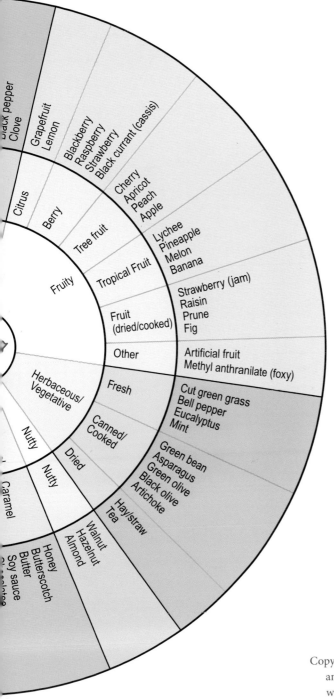

Black pepper
Clove
Grapefruit
Lemon
Blackberry
Raspberry
Strawberry
Black currant (cassis)
Cherry
Apricot
Peach
Apple
Citrus
Berry
Tree fruit
Lychee
Pineapple
Melon
Banana
Fruity
Tropical Fruit
Strawberry (jam)
Raisin
Prune
Fig
Fruit
(dried/cooked)
Other
Artificial fruit
Methyl anthranilate (foxy)
Herbaceous/
Vegetative
Fresh
Cut green grass
Bell pepper
Eucalyptus
Mint
Canned/
Cooked
Green bean
Asparagus
Green olive
Black olive
Artichoke
Nutty
Dried
Hay/straw
Tea
Nutty
Walnut
Hazelnut
Almond
Caramel
Honey
Butterscotch
Butter
Soy sauce

Wine Tasting: The Basics

Sip

At last, the moment you've been waiting for: when wine meets taste buds! Taste buds reside throughout your mouth: on the side, underneath, and on the tip of your tongue, and also in the back of your throat. The different areas are sensitive to different flavors. Swallowing the wine too quickly doesn't allow time for the wine to linger on your taste buds.

So take your time to enjoy the wine!

- Taste once, twice, three times to fully experience the flavor.
- As you sip the wine, draw a little bit of air into your mouth. This will further aerate the wine and bring out more of the flavors.

The "finish"

The aftertaste of wine is referred to as the "finish." In high-quality wine, the aftertaste can linger from one to three minutes. After you have sipped and swallowed, notice how long the finish lingers in your mouth.

People perceive four kinds of tastes: sweet, sour, bitter, and salty (but wine contains no salt). You can learn to determine various sensations of taste.

What are tannins in wine?

- Tannins are a "textural" element that can create a dry sensation in the mouth.
- Tannins are a naturally occurring polyphenol (an organic component) found in plants, seeds, bark, wood, leaves and fruit skins.
- As a typical component of wine, tannins add bitterness, astringency and complexity to the wine. Tannins are mostly found in red wines. Some white wines have tannins after being aged in oak barrels.

HIGH-TANNIN VARIETALS:	LOW-TANNIN VARIETALS:
Nebbiolo	Barbera
Cabernet Sauvignon	Zinfandel
Tempranillo	Pinot Noir
Petit Verdot	Grenache
Petit Sirah	Merlot

What tannins do for wine:

- Preserve wine for long-term aging.

- Provide "structure" in red wine. Too little structure will cause wine to seem "flabby" or lacking in acidity. Tannins create "balance."

- Their astringency extends a wine's flavor "finish," i.e., how long the flavor lingers after you have swallowed a sip. You may hear wine pros refer to the "long finish on the end." This comes from the tannins.

Savor

The last step in adventurous wine tasting is to take a few moments to think about what you just experienced.

Consider:

- Was this wine light-, medium- or full-bodied? Compare it to skim milk, whole milk, or heavy cream.

- For white wine: did you taste the acidity?

- For red wine: was the tannin too strong (or "astringent"), pleasing, or missing altogether?

- How long did the aftertaste (or finish) last?

- What was the strongest flavor that you registered? Sugar? Fruit? Acid? Tannin?

- Was the wine balanced (acidity, tannin, sweetness)?

- What kind of food might you enjoy with this wine?
- Is this wine worth the asking price?
- Is this wine your "style," and did you like it?

During wine tasting the person pouring the wine may mention what you should expect to smell and taste. Don't be abashed if the wine pro says, "This wine has a slight hint of apricot and black currant…" and you don't taste these flavors. Worry not if you taste almonds instead of apricots. No two people have the same taste buds!

If you feel a bit intimidated by the supreme confidence conveyed by those who describe the fine intricacies of wine bouquets and tastes, you are not alone. Remember, you may smell different aromas and taste different flavors than the person pouring the wine. You are entitled to your own opinion and your own experience; the most important thing is that *you enjoy* the taste! This *is* the Snob Free adventure of wine tasting, after all!

How do you know if the wine is ready and a good one for you?

When all the elements of the wine are in balance **to your individual taste!**

You get to decide!

5 Common Sensory Descriptors

FRUITY
  citrus — grapefruit, lemon
  berry — blackberry, raspberry, strawberry, black currant (cassis)
  tree fruit — cherry, apricot, peach, apple
  tropical fruit — pineapple, melon, banana
  dried fruit — strawberry jam, raisin, prune, fig

VEGETATIVE
  fresh — stemmy, cut green grass, bell pepper, eucalyptus, mint
  canned-cooked — green beans, asparagus,
    green olive, black olive, artichoke
  dried — hay-straw, tea, tobacco

NUTTY   walnut, hazelnut, almond

CARAMELIZED
  honey, butterscotch, butter, soy sauce, chocolate, molasses

WOODY   vanilla, cedar, oak, smoky, burnt toast, charred, coffee

EARTHY   dusty, mushroom, musty (mildew), moldy cork

CHEMICAL
  petroleum — tar, plastic, kerosene, diesel
  sulfur — rubbery, garlic, skunk, cabbage, burnt match, wet wool,
    wet dog
  papery — wet cardboard
  pungent — acetic acid (vinegar)
  other — soapy, fishy

PUNGENT
  hot — alcohol

  cool — menthol

MICROBIOLOGICAL   yeast, sauerkraut,
sweaty, horsey, mousey

FLORAL   orange blossom, rose, violet, geranium

SPICY   cloves, black pepper, licorice, anise

6   Annual Growth Cycle of Grapevines

Grapevine and fruit

The grapevine growth cycle begins in the spring with "bud break" and peaks with harvest and "leaf fall" in autumn, and ends with "dormancy" in the winter. These stages of the grape growth cycle are more than horticultural subtitles; each represents a scene of visual delight as you drive through the Napa and Sonoma wine country. The green of bud break in many cases is accompanied by vast fields of yellow mustard. The vines develop nuanced shades of green in orderly rows that create breathtaking lush patchwork quilts in the hills and valleys. And prior to dormancy, the wine country is awash with shades of gold, red and brown that lend a warm glow through the harvest season.

For wine making, each step in this glorious cycle is important to the development of the grapes. The type of climate (warmer or cooler), and the different varietal characteristics determine the duration of each stage in the growth cycle of various wine crops.

Bud Break

Grapes start their annual cycle in the spring with bud break. This stage begins around March, when temperatures rise above 50° F. Vines are usually pruned during the winter months, in January and February. The start of bud break begins with a "bleeding" of the vine. When the soil begins to warm, water pushed up through the root system becomes evident, as it comes through cuts in the stem that were made during winter pruning. One vine can bleed more than a gallon of water!

Small buds on the vine swell, and shoots appear. Leaves sprout, photosynthesis begins and the plant has more energy to grow. A month after bud break starts, plant growth speeds up to reach an incredible rate of one to two inches per day.

Bud break and frost damage

If the early spring brings temperatures below freezing, vineyard managers are known to take aggressive action to prevent frost damage to young shoots.

Wind machines thirty feet tall, with 18-foot propellers, are used to mix the warmer air from above the ground (the inversion layer) with cooler air around the vines. This prevents the young buds from freezing. One wind machine can provide an average 1 to 3° F of warming for about 10 to 12 acres of vineyard, thus preventing frost damage to the grapevines.

Flowering

Forty to eighty days after bud break, small flower clusters appear when average daily temperatures reach around 59 to 68°. Typically, this takes place around May. After flowering clusters appear, they begin to grow and become larger. At this stage, pollination takes place.

Now you will have to forgive my childlike excitement about getting to use a word that biology teachers don't bat an eye about:

Hermaphrodite [her-maph-ro-dite] — noun
Biology. An organism, as an earthworm or plant, having normally both the male and female organs of generation. [www.Dictionary.com]

Most grapevines are *hermaphroditic*, containing both male stamens and female ovaries. There, I said it! Grapevines are able to *self-pollinate* without the help of bees or wasps.

Wind and insects play a very small role in the pollination process. As the pollen fertilizes the ovary, it produces a seed, which eventually grows into a berry. At this stage, the future crop of grapes will begin to form. During this time, poor weather may also play a role as wind, freezing temperatures and rain can hinder the flowering process.

Fruit Set

After fertilization, fruit begins to form around the seed. This will take place around May. **Flowering and fruit set** are very critical stages for wine production. The new year's crop of fruit production is dependent on these two stages and the weather. If flowers don't get fertilized or if they fall off the vine the grape yield for the current year will be sub-optimal.

Other factors that can negatively affect the health of the vineyard are high temperatures, low humidity and lack of water. The number of flowers that get fertilized will play a significant role in seed production and size of fruit. A berry without a seed will be smaller than a berry with a seed. This inconsistency of fruit size may cause production issues during the wine making process.

Veraison

Grape berries are hard and green following the fruit set stage. They contain very little sugar. At this point they have grown to half their final size. The **veraison** stage signals the start of the ripening process, around the end of July and into August.

At this stage, the color of the grapes begins to change from green to red/black or yellow/green, depending on varietal type. The berries soften as they increase in sugar content, decrease in acidity and begin to grow dramatically.

Inconsistent berry color is iconic of the veraison stage. The clusters of berries in the outer canopy that are most exposed to the sun's heat will turn their final color first.

Also during veraison, the cane of the vines begins to turn from green to brown and become hard. The vine begins to store some of its energy production for reserves that become the next cycle of growth. For high-quality wine, an earlier veraison is considered ideal.

Harvest

High season in the wine country is harvest time. Vineyards are abuzz with activity. Grape clusters are removed from the vine and transported to the "crush pad" of the winery to start the wine making production process. Usually this begins in September and may last through October. In years of

variable weather, harvest may begin in late August or early September.

The wine maker and vineyard manager determine when the grapes are ready to be picked. They consider sugar levels, measured by a refractometer (see page 35) using a Brix scale, the taste of the grapes, the acidity or pH level, the threat of poor weather conditions and the potential for vine diseases in making their decisions.

As grapes ripen on the vine, sugar levels, tartaric acid and pH increase, while malic acids decrease. Tannins also develop, which affect aromas and flavors in the wine.

Leaf Fall and Winter Dormancy

After the harvest, the vines will continue a growth process of photosynthesis. This stage creates reserves that are stored in the vine's root system and trunk. The chlorophyll in the leaves will break down and the leaves will turn from green to yellow and brown.

Following the first frost in October or November, the leaves will begin to fall. **Winter dormancy** will begin when most of the leaves have fallen from the vines.

7 The Wine Making Process

I love exposure to the "behind the scenes" mechanics of wine production. After patiently tending the grapes from the start of bud break through the ripening process, the grapes are transformed into wine through a methodical process. I'm amazed at the countless decisions that go into wine production, from the fermentation process through bottling and corking. Here's a quick tour of what happens after the grapes are picked.

Wine Making Production Overview

After harvest in the vineyard, grapes typically go through the following wine making process:

1 Destemming: This process separates vine stems from the grapes.

Mechanical fingers separate stems and push destemmed grapes through cylinder.

Destemmed grapes are expelled through holes in the cylinder.

2 First Press: In a bladder press, a canvas balloon, through a contraction and expansion process, squeezes the juice out of the grapes.

3 Fermentation: Grape juice sugar is converted into alcohol.

Bladder press

- Red wine is fermented with skins, pulp, juices and seeds. The result is called "must."

- White wine is separated from skins before fermentation.

- Yeast is added or develops; this modifies aromas and flavors, as well as ferments the grape juice.

4 Barrel Aging: Wine is stored in oak barrels and/or steel or concrete tanks to age.

5 Malolactic Fermentation (ML) (Secondary Fermentation): Bacteria may be added to oak barrels to induce malolactic fermentation, in order to manipulate the acidic structure and make the wine taste smooth.

Destemmed grapes in fermentation bins

6 Racking: Yeast sediment (called lees) is separated from wine after fermentation by gravity.

7 Bottling: Wine is bottled with or without filtration. This is a decision of the wine maker. "Bottle aging" refers to the continued aging and evolution of wine once it has been bottled.

What is wine — technically speaking?

Yeast + Glucose (sugar) $\longrightarrow$
Ethanol (alcohol) + Carbon Dioxide = WINE

Yeast is added (naturally or artificially) to glucose (sugar). Many grapes have natural yeast on their stems, but in varying quantities.

A wine maker will usually add yeast to speed up and control the fermentation process.

The yeast cells convert sugars to ethanol and carbon dioxide, thus creating heat, more yeast and flavor.

The alcohol that results from fermentation will contain 9%-16% ethanol. High sugar content must be present for fermentation to progress to the desired result.

Sugar and wine

No doubt you have noticed that the sweet taste of wines varies. This is no accident. Wine makers carefully gauge the level of sugar in ripened grapes to determine when to pick them. And they could not do this with much precision if it weren't for the development of the hydrometer, invented by a 19th-century Austrian scientist, Adolf Brix. (Gadget alert!) The hydrometer, used in chemistry labs, enabled sugar measurement in liquid. Not only is sugar measured by taste, but also by the Brix scale.

The Brix scale indicates the percent of sugar by weight in unfermented juice. These days, however, the instrument used in the field is a hand-held device that refracts light, called a refractometer.

Harvest often takes place when the Brix sugar level reaches between 22 and 27 on the Brix measurement scale.

The sweetness of wine can be determined by several factors that include the amount of sugar in the wine and the level of alcohol, acids and

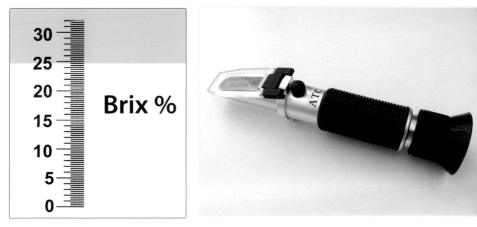

Brix Scale reading 25   Refractometer

tannins present. Sugar and alcohol add to the sweetness of a wine, while acids and bitter tannins detract from the sweetness. Part of the great art of wine making is the balancing of these factors.

A dry wine may taste sweet if the alcohol level is high. Many of the world's great wines have high levels of residual sugar, which are carefully balanced with additional acidity to produce a wine considered "harmonious." Ironically, consumers often assume that a very sweet wine is low-caliber.

There are over 4,000 varieties of **vitis vinifera**, which is the Latin name for the grape most often used for wine making production. The variance and quality of wines derive from the type of grape varietal used and from the **qualities of soil, wind, sun, heat and elevation** — also known as **terroir** — that make up the climate of the vineyard.

Preparation for wine making

When the grapes are picked — whether for white or red wine — and taken to the winery, specific steps are taken to ensure good wine making. The grapes may be treated with sulfur dioxide upon arriving at the winery. This is called "sulfating," and inhibits the growth of any unwanted microorganisms.

Cleanliness and sanitation must be top priority in all wine making facilities. All equipment is sanitized with an approved solution, and then rinsed with water. Then the same surfaces are treated with an anti-

bacterial sulfite solution. To rid all equipment of any excess sulfite on surfaces that have contact with grapes, everything is again rinsed with water. It takes approximately ten gallons of water to make one gallon of wine! The largest use of water is in sanitizing the bottles during the bottling phase of production.

White Wine Production

Destemming and pressing grapes

White wine grapes are brought to the winery, destemmed and inserted into a press. This is usually a "bladder press," a huge balloon that expands and contracts slowly and gently to press the juice from the grapes, leaving the skins behind.

The juice is then pumped into holding tanks and chilled; any sediment drops to the bottom of the tank. After the sediment is removed, the wine is ready to be fermented with yeast.

White wine fermentation

The juice is moved to fermentation tanks, yeast is added and thus the conversion process of juice into wine begins. A few small wineries use the natural yeast in the grapes to begin this process, while most others insert commercial yeast because it produces predictable results. The juice is then moved into large vats where the wine maker can ensure that no air is present. Often dry ice or nitrogen is used to cover the vat to keep out air so fewer bacteria can grow. Fermentation will take place over a 10-to-25-day period. A constant temperature of 55° F is maintained, so the yeast cells can grow and produce the gentle flavors and aromas associated with white wines and cold ferments.

Malolactic fermentation

Most wines fermented in oak barrels will go through a secondary fermentation process known as **malolactic fermentation, or ML**. *This bacterial process*, where **malic acid is converted to lactic acid**, manipulates the acidity in the wine. As a result, the "texture" of the wine changes from crisp and light to a creamier buttery flavor. ML bacteria is often introduced into the oak barrel to start the process.

Red Wine Production

Cold soaking or maceration

After the usual destemming process, the grapes are crushed, resulting in "**must**," a combination of grapes, skins, seeds and juice. The "must" is moved into bins, where fermentation takes place and the wine will "cold soak" for several days.

It is this "**cold soak**" stage that gives red wine its color. Prior to this process, all varietal wine grape juice is clear in color. (Before I learned this, I thought grape juice was all purple, like what's sold in the store!) Cold soaking for eight hours or one full day results in a rosé wine. Cold soaking for a few weeks results in red wine. This is when the wine gets many of its flavors and final color.

The further addition of sulfur dioxide may be necessary to stop the growth of any wild yeast or bacteria that has not been killed by sulfation at the beginning of the wine making process.

Fermentation

After several days of cold soaking, yeast is introduced to the "must" and

Pumping over the must

fermentation may begin. At this stage in the process, carbon dioxide will push the "**must**" (**or grape skins**) to the top of the bin, creating a "**cap**."

"Punching down" or "pumping over" the must

The contact the grape skins have with the juice enhances wine color and tannins. To maintain contact with the skins and juice, the "**cap**" is "**punched down**" at least three or four times a day to mix the juice with the skins. This is done manually at smaller wineries or by "**pumping over**" the juice on top of the cap, and by hydraulic pumps at larger wineries with large fermentation tanks. Aggressive mishandling of the cap results in harsh, sharp-tasting wines. (Certain types of pumps that transfer energy to the liquid, such as impeller pumps, are the worst "blenders.")

**Ask to see the "punch down" process when you visit small wineries in September or October. It's quite exciting to watch!

Continued pressing and settling

Red wine will ferment for about 10 to 14 days. It will take this long for the yeast to convert sugar to alcohol and carbon dioxide. The higher the desired sugar content, the longer the fermentation will take. A lack of cloudiness in the "must" is one sign that fermentation is complete. When the Brix refractometer reads 0% sugar, fermentation is complete.

After cold soaking is complete, the red wine skins are pressed in a bladder press one more time to extract all the juice. The result is dry raisined skins, which can now be turned into mulch and put back into the vineyard. The wine is then set aside for a few more days for the sediment and dead yeast cells (the lees) to settle at the bottom of the tank. These are then separated and then discarded.

Aging in oak barrels

While white wine may be aged in oak, steel or concrete, red wine is moved only to oak barrels for aging. Red wines may be aged from many months up to eight to ten years; the average red wine is aged about three to five years before release. The oak barrel aging process allows some oxygen to enter the process, and any water and some alcohol inside the barrel to evaporate. Acidity decreases, and some clarification of the wine will take place. Oak barrel aging further enhances the flavor and aroma of the wine.

The first two years of use of an oak barrel are the most potent for enhancing the taste of the wine. After three or four uses, the oak barrel is considered "neutral," i.e., it will no longer impart flavor to the wine. Neutral oak is used by wineries for aging wine when the wine maker does not want the barrel to impart flavor.

Sparkling Wines

Sparkling wines are produced in the same fashion as other white wines until fermentation is complete (i.e., grapes are pressed and fermented, then transferred to barrels.)

Adding carbonation

The production of sparkling wine involves the addition of sugar and more yeast to start a bottle fermentation. Airtight seals cap the bottles so that the carbon dioxide that creates carbonation remains trapped inside. The yeast is terminated or stopped, and the need to get rid of excess sediment leads to a method of extraction called *méthode champenoise*. The yeast does its job fermenting the "dosage" of sugar creating the bubbles. The excess yeast is then stopped by cooling and placing the bottles at an angle to collect the yeast sediment. Freezing the neck allows a "plug" of yeast to be removed and a cork is then added. The exact steps in Méthode Champenoise are explained below.

Méthode Champenoise

It would seem that one would need a magic wand to extract sediment and yeast from a closed bottle without losing carbonation. How can this be done? Enter **Méthode Champenoise**. The magic is in the storage of the bottles and the subsequent extraction of the unwanted material in the form of ice plugs. Pure genius!

1 Specifically designed racks are used to store bottles at an angle. This is called "riddling." (*See picture below.*)

2 The bottles are turned one-quarter turn, at least twice a day. Eventually the sediment will settle in the neck of the bottles.

3 When the sediment is ready to be extracted, the bottles are sent through a disgorging line.

4 The neck of each bottle is frozen so that small ice plugs form in the very end of the bottle.

5 The pressurized cap is removed and the pressure of the carbon dioxide forces the ice plug out of the bottle. The sediment that has become frozen in the ice plug is thus removed.

6 A small amount of wine is added back into the bottle, which is corked to prevent any carbon dioxide from escaping.

7 A small wire cage is added over the cork for safety before the foil is added to the top of the bottle.

Fortified Wines

Grapes for fortified wines are left on the vine for an additional period so that the sugar level increases beyond 27 Brix. These excessively ripe grapes are processed in the same fashion as red wine. Fortified wines then have extra alcohol added as part of the fermentation process. Port is a popular example of a fortified wine. Extra alcohol is added to the wine during the fermentation process.

Fortifying with additional spirits

Once fermentation is half-completed, additional alcohol, brandy or grape spirits are added. This adds more alcohol by volume, and in the case of Port, can equal approximately 17%-24% total alcohol. The alcohol level becomes too high for yeast to survive.

A Brief History of Port

Being a fan of Port, I thought this was interesting…

Port and Sherry became more popular in England after a treaty in 1703 allowed merchants to import wine from Spain and Portugal with lower taxes. Later, war with France kept English wine drinkers from consuming French wine, so the Spanish and Portuguese imports became even more popular.

The long sea trips from foreign shores to England often resulted in spoiled wine. The solution: the addition of extra alcohol or brandy to improve the wines' longevity. Over time, the English grew to enjoy wine fortified with additional alcohol.   *(Continued on next page)*

Later, in the early 1800s, grape growers began applying new methods; grapes were allowed to ripen on the vine longer, producing sweeter wine. This became very popular in England, along with the extra fortification with brandy for the sea trip. Over the years, more grape spirits were added and the popularity of Port grew. Wine making methods evolved over time to include earlier fortification during the fermentation process to produce sweeter wine.

Wine Texture

Why is wine texture important in wine tasting?

Texture is another dimension to wine tasting, as are aroma and flavor. Texture can seem like one of those snob words that is often used in the wine tasting arena. While we think of "texture" as something we feel with our hands, in wine tasting you can actually feel the texture with your tongue.

What do people mean when they talk about the texture of a wine?

When the word "texture" is used to describe a wine, it refers to a physical sensation on the palate, not dissimilar to the description of texture in tasting food. The physical sensation in your mouth would be the texture of the wine. Most texture discussions involve drinking red wine, because of the presence of tannin. Tannin has certain physical characteristics ranging from smooth to somewhat "chewy," "astringent," and even "coarse." Here are some words that describe the texture of wine. Take a sip of red wine and try these descriptors on for size while you savor the taste.

Wine Texture Descriptors

Creamy	Tingly	Chamois
Viscous	Mouthcoat	Satiny
Thin	Rich	Metallic
Watery	Puckery	Sour
Prickly	Silky	Soapy

Ingredients that contribute to wine texture: tannin, alcohol, and sugars

As mentioned above, tannin in red wine contributes significantly to texture. Compare, for example, the silky tannins of an aged red wine to the astringent tannins of a young red wine that hasn't been aged enough.

Alcohol has an important influence on texture, by way of the sweet, syrupy glycerol it generates. In general, higher-alcohol wines have more glycerol than lower-alcohol wines. Alcohol adds viscosity to a wine. Compare a wine with 14% alcohol to one with about 12.5%. You can feel the physical difference.

Additionally, depending on the specific type of varietal, different types of sugar molecules linked together to form complex chains can add various levels of richness to a wine's texture through their molecular configuration.

Buttery flavor explained

Malolactic fermentation produces buttery flavors and creamy textures. As stated earlier, this involves the transformation of malic acid into lactic acid. Malic acid is quite tart and bright, like the feel you get when you bite into a green apple. Lactic acid is milder and softer; think milk.

After ML, acidity is reduced, and the texture of the wine is creamier. The ML process produces a byproduct, diacetyl, which gives nutty and buttery flavors to a wine. You'll recognize the smell of diacetyl at movie theaters since it is used in products to make them butter-flavored.

While ML is standard for all red wines, many wine makers do not allow all white wines to go through this process. According to some wine makers, white wines are intended to be fresh and crisp, and so the presence of malic acid is beneficial. Thus, some wines do not undergo the ML process, or only a portion (sometimes only 30%) of the wine is permitted to go through malolactic fermentation to maintain acidity and balance in the wine.

Separation and bottling

When fermentation is complete (usually decided by a taste test conducted by the wine maker), the wine is separated from the dead yeast cells, called the "lees." The wine can then be chilled to create more "clarification" before bottling. Larger wineries have their own bottling equipment, but smaller wineries typically contract out the bottling line.

Picture this: An 18-wheel truck backs into the winery, the bottling line enclosed in the truck's trailer. The winery provides the labels, bottles, foil and wine and in a few hours, a third of the winery's production can be bottled right there on the truck.

Wine Clarification

Wine clarification is the process by which suspended matter in the wine is removed just before bottling. This may include substances like dead yeast cells (lees), bacteria, proteins, and tannins, as well as pieces of grape skin and pulp.

The process of clarification may include refrigeration, pasteurization, filtration, barrel maturation and "racking," which means moving wine from one barrel to another for the purpose of cleaning unwanted matter out from the old barrel. Racking mechanically clarifies wine through gravity and sedimentation.

8 Use of Oak Barrels to Age Wine

Storing wine in oak barrels has occurred for thousands of years, even during the Roman Empire. Over time, wine makers discovered that beyond just storing wine, the taste of the wine itself was improved by contact with the oak barrels.

Robert Mondavi, legendary founder of Robert Mondavi Winery, began experimenting with oak barrel storage, using French, American and Hungarian oak barrels during the 1960s. His experiments with oak barrel storage widely influenced wine makers in the United States.

Storing wine in oak barrels has a significant impact on the final wine product. It is similar to a "tea bag effect"; the amount of time wine is stored in oak affects its color, tannin structure, flavor and texture.

Wine may be placed in oak during or after fermentation for the aging and maturation process. Wine that is aged and matured in new oak barrels absorbs more of the oak flavor than wine fermented in neutral oak barrels (four or more years old).

Oak barrel effects on wine taste

There is a porous characteristic of oak that allows small amounts of evaporated liquid to escape. This is referred to as "**The Angel's Share**." The low amounts of oxygen that pass through the barrel can act as a softening agent on the tannins in the wine. Most barrels containing 59.3 gallons of wine will lose five to six gallons a year during the aging process due to evaporation. That liquid consists mostly of alcohol and water. Anticipating this, wine makers set aside extra wine to "top off" the barrels periodically, to fill the space caused by the evaporation. Storing oak barrels in humid environments such as wine caves causes less evaporation.

Toasting of oak barrels

Most visitors to the wine country find it fascinating to learn that oak barrels are "toasted." Yes, fire is applied to the oak at the barrel factories, which are called cooperages. Toasting is a key step in mellowing the wood's harsh tannins and reducing the raw oak flavors, in addition to carmelizing sugars in the oak sap, creating new flavor enhancement. The markings on the barrels tell whether the toasting has been light, medium, medium plus, or heavy and whether the heads (round sides at each end) of the barrel have been toasted.

Samples showing different levels of toasting of oak barrels

Differences between French and American oak

French oak barrels are the preferred choice of wine makers in the United States and elsewhere. French oak has a tighter grain than American oak, due to cooler average temperatures in France. This allows a slower

Aroma descriptors associated with oak barrel toasting

The following words are used as descriptors of the effects of oak barrel toasting and its impact on the wine during aging:

vanilla	allspice	brown sugar
caramel	cinnamon	nutmeg
dark chocolate	butterscotch	honey
cocoa	clove	cream
toast	smoke	hazelnut
coffee	tobacco	espresso
mocha	coconut	roasted coffee bean
toasted almond	French vanilla	

integration of flavors in the wine. It is, however, considerably more costly:

- French oak barrel = $1,000 to $1,500 per barrel (depending on which forest in France it comes from)
- American oak barrel = $600 per barrel

American oak tends to have more flavored sweetness and vanilla because the oak has more lactones. Wine makers will choose American oak for more bold and powerful red wines.

Another major difference between French and American oak is the preparation of the wood by the cooperage, the place that makes the barrels. French oak must be split along the grain; this makes the wood less watertight. The wood is "seasoned" and aged for 2 to 2½ years in the open air. Since French oak must be split in a certain manner, only 25% of the tree can be used for oak barrels, which contributes to its cost. The average age of a French oak tree harvested for use in creating wine barrels is 170 years.

American oak has a wider grain than French oak, so more of the tree can be used for making barrels. Hence, it's more economical. It also has a quicker release of aromas and faster oxidation, making it a better choice for shorter aging and faster maturations.

9　How to Read a U.S. Wine Label

TERM	WHAT IT MEANS
Winery/Maker	Producer of wine.
Estate Bottled	The U.S. government department of Alcohol, Tobacco, Tax and Trade Bureau (also called the TTB) has set certain requirements for the wine industry's use of the word "estate" on labels in the U.S.:

    + 100% of the wine must be made from grapes that are either grown on the land owned by the winery, or wholly controlled by the winery. (Many wineries source grapes from other vineyards than their own or from other growers.)

    + The estate vineyards must be inside a designated American Viticultural Area (AVA). The vineyard and the winery must be in the same AVA.

    + The winery must press the grapes and ferment them, as well as bottle the wine at their own vineyard or "crush pad" location.

    + The wine must not leave that location at time during the production process, including the bottling stage.

NOTE: This wine label is fictitious.

MARLANDY
WINERY
— Winery/Maker

RESERVE — Estate or Reserve

RUTHERFORD, NAPA VALLEY — Appellation Region

CHARDONNAY — Varietal

2014 — Vintage

Bottler — Bottled by Hyman, Inc., Rutherford, CA ◆ 750 ml ◆ Alc. 15% by vol. — Alcohol content

Bottle size

Reserve

MARLANDY
WINERY

RESERVE

RUTHERFORD, NAPA VALLEY
PINOT NOIR
2014
Bottled by Hyman, Inc., Rutherford, CA • 750 ml • Alc, 15% by vol.

In some European countries the use of the term "reserve" is strictly regulated, but in the U.S. it is a marketing term with no formal or legal restrictions.

Use of the word "reserve" on a bottle of wine implies that it is of higher quality than other wines from the same producer.

Wine makers traditionally "reserve" grapes or wine from their best tasting barrels. They may also age the wine longer than other wines from the same vineyard.

* Be aware that some large U.S. wineries that produce hundreds of thousands of cases of wine place the word "reserve" on their labels for marketing purposes. This has caused some confusion among consumers, who are not aware that this is used as a marketing term with no limits to its meaning.

Varietal

To carry the name of a varietal on a label such as Cabernet Sauvignon, Merlot, Chardonnay, etc., the wine must be made of at least 75% of that varietal. If it has less than 75% of the varietal, it is considered a "blend."

Vintage

The vintage represents the year the grapes were harvested (not bottled).

Appellation Region

American Viticultural Area in which the grapes were grown. At least 85% of the grapes grown for the wine must come from the appellation stated on the bottle.

TERM	WHAT IT MEANS
Bottler	The name of the bottling company, which may be different than the wine producer.
Bottle Size	The amount of milliliters in the bottle.
Alcohol Content	The exact percentage of alcohol content.
Sulfite Declaration	Any wines containing more than 10 parts per million of sulfur dioxide must be labeled "contains sulfites." Wines optionally labeled as "organic" must be free of any artificially added sulfites. Those labeled as "Made with organically grown grapes" will have some sulfites.
Meritage	The word "Bordeaux" cannot be used for wine produced outside the Bordeaux region of France. Hence, the word "Meritage" was created by Chris Consentino for a "Bordeaux Style" blend of wines. Bordeaux blends contain mixtures of Cabernet Sauvignon, Merlot, Cabernet Franc, Petit Verdot, and Malbec. At least 75% of a varietal must be contained in a bottle for that varietal to appear on the label.

10 The World's Most Popular Wines by Region

The following list reflects the most popular wines produced internationally, in order of volume.

	REGION	GRAPES	WINE COLOR
1	**France**	Sauvignon Blanc	○
		Chardonnay	○
		Riesling	○
		Grenache	●
		Pinot Noir	●
		Cabernet Sauvignon	●
		Merlot	●
		Syrah	●
2	**Italy**	Merlot	●
		Sangiovese	●
		Pinot Grigio	○
		Trebbiano	○
3	**Spain**	Tempranillo	●
		Airen	○
4	**United States** (88% from California's 3,700 wineries)	Pinot Noir	●
		Cabernet Sauvignon	●
		Merlot	●
		Zinfandel	●
		Syrah (or Shiraz)	●
		Chardonnay	○
		Sauvignon Blanc	○

	REGION	GRAPES	WINE COLOR
5	**Argentina**	Malbec	●
		Chardonnay	○
6	**Australia**	Syrah (or Shiraz)	●
		Riesling	○
7	**Germany**	Riesling	○
		Pinot Noir	●
		Gewürztraminer	○
		Müller-Thurgau	○
8	**South Africa**	Syrah (or Shiraz)	●
		Cabernet Sauvignon	●
		Pinotage	●
		Merlot	●
		Sauvignon Blanc	○
		Chenin Blanc	○
		Colombard	○
9	**Chile**	Cabernet	●
		Chardonnay	○
10	**Portugal**	Port Grape Varietals	●
		Alvarinho	○

11 Old World, New World – What's The Difference?

Old world wines and new world wines vary in taste. The difference lies in the geography of the vineyard, the climate, the style of wine making, the tradition of wine making in that region and the innovation in wine making techniques used in the process.

Old World	New World
France	United States
Italy	Argentina
Spain	Australia
Germany	South Africa
Austria	Chile
Hungary	New Zealand
Portugal	Anywhere else
Greece	not considered
Romania	"Old World"
Croatia	

Rules for wine making

Old world wines are tied to tradition. Also, there is strict government regulation of what types of wine grapes may be grown in each region and how wine can be made. The government may also tell wine makers how much wine they may produce.

New world wines are made with no government guidelines telling wine makers the types of grapes they may grow, where they can grow or which techniques to use making the wine.

Names and labels on bottles

Old world wines are named after the location of the growing region. Their labels name the region: e.g., Bordeaux, Burgundy, Champagne. "Terroir" is the set of characteristics the geography, geology and climate of a place expresses in its agricultural products, which is considered fundamental in old world wines. In contrast, new world wines are named after the varietal of grapes grown and produced inside the bottle of wine, such as Cabernet Sauvignon, Zinfandel, Merlot, Sauvignon Blanc or Chardonnay.

Style of wine making

Old world wines are more subtle in flavor and aroma. Their colors are more subdued, and they are considered more earthy. New world wines are more intense, have deeper color and their aromas are more likely to be pronounced. They are more fruit forward in style, i.e., the taste of fruit is the first thing you notice when sipping it. New world red wines are typically fuller-bodied.

Old World, New World — What's the Difference?

12   Dispelling Wine Myths and Misconceptions

Myth   **Screw caps go with cheap, poor quality wine**

Screw caps have gotten a bad rap. There is no technical reason wines with a screw cap won't age as well or better than those with a cork.

Needless to say, the cork industry would like consumers to believe otherwise. Entire countries such as Australia and New Zealand, however use screw caps for wine closures.

The fact is that screw caps are more consistent at sealing wine than cork. A study referred to in the highly respected industry magazine *Wine Spectator* (March 31, 2005, pages 59-60,) says that screw caps allow less oxygen to enter the wine bottle: .001 cc's of oxygen per day on average for screw caps, versus .1 to .001 cc's of oxygen per day on average for corks.

Like many businesses, some wineries are interested in lowering the expense of producing wine; steering clear of the rising costs of cork is one way to do that — and then pass the savings on to you. So, while the tradition, drama and romance of popping the cork may diminish when you are opening that screw cap, it may be worth the savings if the wine is one you enjoy. You may drink wine with screw caps with no shame, now that you know the real story. Carry on!

Myth   **Expensive wines are superior in quality and taste**

Sometimes this may be true. However, wine prices are influenced by many factors, such as the image of the winery (a function of the winery's marketing talent and budget), wine ratings, celebrity endorsements, cost per ton of grapes, and supply-and-demand. Additionally, the expense to grow grapes in a highly recognized and celebrated viticultural area contributes to the cost per bottle of wine.

If you like a higher-priced wine and can afford it, by all means, buy it! But don't think that you have to spend a lot of money to get good quality. That's just snob-talk. If a bottle of wine tastes good to you and is priced within your budget, then go for it!

Myth Sweet wines are for beginners, not people with educated palates

Many of the great wines of the world are sweet, such as late harvests, sauternes, ice wines and, of course, celebrated (fortified) Port wines. It comes down to preference. More snob-talk. Just ignore it. Drink the wine that best suits your tastes and don't worry about others' opinions.

Myth Red wines cause more headaches than white wines due to their higher sulfite content

Sulfite (sulfur dioxide) is a preservative found in many foods we eat. Red wines have fewer added sulfites than do white wines. Sulfites in wine do not cause headaches but could cause an asthmatic reaction in those who are allergic.

Research suggests that histamine and tyramine, other chemical substances naturally found in wine, may cause headaches; histamine is the more common source of the problem. It is true that red wine has more histamine than sparkling or white wine.

Headaches when wine tasting are usually caused by dehydration or excessive drinking.

Myth Wines labeled "organic" have no sulfites

All wines naturally contain sulfites, which are produced during the fermentation process. Also, most wine makers will add additional sulfites to prevent oxidation and preserve the wine. The legal maximum sulfite level for the United States is 350 ppm (parts per million). Most wines are in the range of 125 ppm. Organic wine makers do not add additional sulfites to the wine making process. Organic wines with no sulfites added range from 10 to 20 ppm.

Myth — Wine tastes better with age

Most white wines are made for consumption when they are released by the winery. They are already aged in the barrel and the bottle for up to

18 months, and should be consumed within one to three years of release.

Over 90% of red wines are made for drinking within five to eight years of release. Despite the popular belief that most red wines "age gracefully" in the bottle, most red wines will move past their prime if aged in the bottle beyond a reasonable aging time. There are a few wines with concentrated fruits, solid acidity, and structured tannins that will age well in the bottle. These are some of the very best, high-quality and high-priced wines.

Consider these "rules of thumb" rather than hard scientific fact.

Myth — Smell the cork at a restaurant to determine if the wine is bad

Smelling the cork at a restaurant will not give any indication if the wine is bad. It is actually the wine you should smell. Put your nose in the

upper two-thirds of the glass, sniff, and decide if the wine has a bad, unusual or unappealing odor. The condition of the cork should be examined, though. It may have TCA or 6-trichloranisole, for those who took chemistry. TCA is a compound that gets into a cork and exudes a musty odor in the wine. A quick examination of the cork will tell you if it has been damaged or any seepage has occurred. View the cork for logo, name or branding information, and date, if it is an expensive bottle of wine. The information should be consistent with the wine label.

Myth: You should drink different wines with different shaped glasses

Should you drink white wine with a tulip shaped glass and red wine with a bigger glass that aerates the wine? There have been studies on the perception of wine tasting and the shape of the glass. There are, however, no conclusive results showing you should have a specific style of glass for different types of wine. There are many styles of wine glasses, all of which are vessels of pleasure when you pour in your favorite wine. Prepare to meet some opposition to this — especially when visiting wineries. Certain wineries have larger glasses for aerating red wine than the glasses for white wine.

Myth: Syrah (or Shiraz) originated in Persia

Syrah and Shiraz are the same grape, be it from its official home in the Syrah region in the northern portion of the Rhône Valley in Southeastern France, or in its newer homes in Australia, South America, South Africa and in California. The term Shiraz is used most frequently in Australia but also in South America, South Africa and sometimes in the United States. In California it's called Syrah. Any stories you may have heard about the grape varietal being from Persia are simply not accurate. DNA tests at the University of California, Davis, the premier institution of enology, have confirmed the varietal originated in France.

13   Good to Know

I nteresting facts about wine abound. Check these out and impress your
friends and family with your knowledge of the wine industry.

What is enology?

Enology comes from the Greek words for wine and study. Enology is the
science of wine making. The science has its roots thousands of years ago,
when the pleasant effects of alcohol were likely discovered by accidental-
ly eating rotten fruit.

Why are grapevines pruned back to almost bare trunks?

When vineyards "prune hard," leaving just a small number
of buds (about three) on each vine, it enhances the quality

of the grapes produced the following year. Without pruning, vines
would concentrate more of their
energy into producing dense
foliage, with small bunches of
grapes. Not only does this reduce
the crop of grapes, that dense
canopy of leaves can also block the
sun, making the vine more prone
to fungal diseases.

Why are roses planted at the end of rows of grapevines?

Roses function like the "canary in the coal mine." They are susceptible to
the pests and diseases (mildew) that can affect grapevines, so are planted
on the edges of vineyards to be struck first by such damage. This sounds

the alarm for the grape grower to control the problem before it affects the vines. There is another reason roses were planted at the end of vineyard rows. Many years ago, when horses pulled harvesting wagons, roses were planted to serve as a "bumper," to keep the horses from cutting corners and damaging valuable grapevines.

Why and how do modern vineyards use "clone" plants?

Planting from seeds is a very unpredictable process; many seeds never germinate. Most growers want to plant and harvest a consistent grape to ensure the predictability of their crops. Clones enable this consistency. A twig with a bud on it is cut from a "mother" plant that displays desirable characteristics. The twig is then grafted onto a good rootstock and planted, resulting in a genetically identical plant.

Why are barrels shaped with a bulge in the middle?

Their shape makes them easier to roll across cellars, turn, and generally move in any direction. Before forklifts were invented, this was how barrels were repositioned. The only reason barrels have maintained their shape is to maintain tradition, since these days, most barrels are moved with a forklift.

How is wine influenced by the age of the vine?

Let's zip through vine growth to give you some perspective. It takes about three to four years from the time a vine is planted until it bears mature fruit for use in wine. Until then, any grapes produced are discarded. In fact, in many "old world" wine-producing countries, grapevines three years old or younger cannot be made into wine by law. When a vine is about five years old, it can produce what is considered a full crop. From then to about thirty years, the vine is in full production mode. After that, the vine slows down and progressively yields less fruit. Vines can live to be over one hundred years old. However, it is rare to see them reach this age. Certain sub-species of vines (clones) thrive longer than others, such as "old-vine Zinfandel."

Old vines and the soil

It is common wisdom that the soil in vineyards heavily influences the taste and quality of European wine. The essential component of "terroir" (soil, local climate) has a huge impact on grape quality and the distinctiveness of a wine's character. Old vines have deeper complex root structures that interact with microorganisms in the soil differently than do younger grapevines. This supplies the older grapevine with nutrition as well as natural sugars. The rarity and flavor, coupled with smaller yields, explains

the label "Old Vines" as well as the higher prices for the more interesting and complex wine product.

There are a small number of vineyards where the grapevines are 60 to 120 years old. These are called "old vines" and may be labeled as such. "Old vines" have certain characteristics that make them very special:

Root depth As grapevines age, the roots penetrate deeper into the soil and may reach depths of up to 30 feet. At this root depth, the grapes benefit from soil nutrients, minerals and water not necessarily available at more shallow depths. These grapevines will not be affected by yearly rainfall inconsistencies or by soil nutrient and mineral deficiencies. Their rootstocks will be very thick.

Berry size As grapevines increase in age, reaching beyond 25 years, the berries become smaller. This is natural to older vines. Many wineries will replant at this point to increase yield size and skin-to-juice ratios. Most of the color and aromas come from the skin of the grape. Older vines produce a much richer aroma and flavor as well as a deeper wine color.

Lower yields of fruit Energy levels tend to drop off as grapevines age. They produce fewer vines, smaller clusters and smaller grapes, which also equals more skin-to-juice ratio. The energy of the plant is concentrated on smaller quantities of grapes. This translates into wine flavors that are more complex.

Are ratings important in purchasing wine?

Only a small number of wineries submit their wines for ratings. Judging wine is a very subjective experience. Just as talent show judges don't agree on scores, often wine judges don't agree with one another about the quality of a particular wine.

Also, even though a wine may be highly rated, it may not necessarily be to your liking, which should be the only criterion for your purchasing decision. Purchase one bottle of a highly rated wine to see if the critic's judgment agrees with your taste. That way you'll know if multiple bottles of the same wine are a good deal for you.

If you are purchasing for a friend or family member whom you know likes a particular varietal that doesn't appeal to you, then a good rating can be a distinguishing factor; at least you know that a knowledgeable wine taster thought that vintage and varietal was better than others.

Why is it important to let red wines "breathe"?

Red table wines generally benefit if uncorked and decanted, and then allowed to stand at least twenty minutes before serving.

decant [de•cant] — verb
gradually pour (liquid, typically wine or a solution) from one container into another, especially without disturbing the sediment. [www.Dictionary.com]

Exposure to oxygen — or **oxidation** — activates the development of the bouquet and aroma, and gives depth and smoothness to the wine. In contrast to simply removing the cork, when the bottle is decanted (especially into a broad-based decanter) the wine has more contact with air and hence absorbs more oxygen.

Good to Know

What accounts for the wide range of wine prices for the same varietal?

Several factors enter into the price of a bottle of wine. Two words capture the most important factor in wine cost: real estate. The location and value of the land and "terroir" where the grapes are grown enter into what the wine maker must invest. Excellent vineyards are a limited resource and, therefore, great grapes from those vineyards typically have a greater cost.

Also, superior wine making skill and talent produces great wine. Nothing can replace the expertise of the wine maker who knows how to cope with weather challenges, determine best production and aging methods, and create a great quality product. Another factor influencing wine cost is the duration of the aging process. Last, the two fundamental dynamics affecting the price of any product in the marketplace are brand marketing and, as our friends from Economics 101 say: supply and demand.

What's the typical pest that affects wine grapes?

Phylloxera, a tiny aphid-like insect, has played havoc in the wine industry in America and Europe during the last 150 years. It was introduced to Europe because a few English botanists brought home American vines in the 1850s. By 1886, Phylloxera had destroyed more than 70% of the European vines, mostly in France. After many experiments, a solution was created: European vines grafted onto American rootstocks were found to be more resistant. The American rootstock had evolved to be resistant because the vines excrete a sticky sap that repels the bug. As a result, hybridization became the method of choice in combating Phylloxera by the end of the 19th century.

Currently, there is no specific cure to combat Phylloxera and vineyards can still contract the pest, despite the fact that most vineyards in the U.S. use American rootstock with European varieties grafted onto it.

14   Shipping Wine Home

Each state is like a separate country when it comes to wine shipping to consumers. There are approximately ten states that have special restrictions for shipping wine from California. Prohibitions and reciprocity agreements vary and change over time, so this list evolves. Most medium-size and large wineries that distribute wine to other states are prohibited from shipping wine directly to:

Alabama	Oklahoma
Arkansas	Pennsylvania
Delaware	South Dakota
Kentucky	Utah
Mississippi	

State restrictions are generally prompted by economic issues. If out-of state wineries ship directly to the consumer, in-state distributors miss the revenue opportunity on those sales. Most larger wineries are required to pay a license fee for the privilege of shipping to specific states. Most states' wine shipping laws were created in 1933 at the end of Prohibition; each state determined and continues to determine its own laws for the transport of alcohol. (Most smaller wineries can ship to most states.)

You have a few options for getting wine you buy home from wineries. The winery staff will tell you if their winery ships to your state. If there are restrictions, you may want to ship the wine to a neighboring state that you visit frequently.

- Some wineries have developed relationships with third-party shippers who ship to restricted states.

- Another option is to purchase a wine shipper (cardboard box with a foam insert to protect the wine) from the winery and take it to a retail shipping location near where you are staying. Some shippers may be able to ship to a restricted state, even though a winery cannot do so.

- The most efficient and least expensive way to get wine home with you is to purchase a wine shipper at the winery that holds 12 bottles and bring it with you to the airport as checked luggage. Note: Don't tape the box closed before you get to the airport, since the airline staff will want to see what is inside. By taking the box on the plane, it won't be stuck in a hot warehouse waiting for shipment. Typically, airlines apply their usual luggage fees to such cargo. A couple of airlines do not charge for luggage. Your wine will be fine in this shipping process; thousands of people who visit the wine country each year take wine home this way, with no damage.

15   Math of Wine Making

1 **cluster of grapes** = approximately 75 to 100 grapes

1 **glass** of wine = 8 clusters of grapes

1 **bottle** contains:

- 32 clusters of grapes
- 750 milliliters of wine
- about 2.4 pounds of grapes (39 ounces)
- 25.6 ounces of wine
- 4 glasses of wine (or 6, if leaving room to swirl)

1 **vine** annually produces

- 4 to 6 bottles of wine or 16 to 24 glasses

1 **case** of wine includes:

- a dozen 750 milliliter bottles
- 307.2 ounces
- from 30 pounds of grapes
- 48 glasses of wine

1 **standard oak barrel** of wine holds:

- 295 bottles of wine (59.5 gallons) made from 740 pounds of grapes
- approximately 24.6 cases of wine
- 1,180 glasses of wine

1 **acre of vineyard land** can give the grower:

- 4 tons of grapes (average)
- 500 gallons of juice (approximate)
- or 13.5 barrels
- close to 3,958 bottles of wine

16　　　Fun Facts

1. The kitchen is usually too warm to store wine safely.

2. You may be surprised to know that even the warmest setting in your refrigerator isn't good for wine storage; it's too cold! The best place is in a basement or a garage, where the temperature is no higher than 65° F.

3. California, New York, and Florida lead the U.S. in wine consumption.

4. All juice from wine grapes is clear. Red wine is produced as a result of the contact between red grapes and their fermenting juice; this extracts the red color and the complexity of taste from the grape skins. White wines have no contact with their grape skins during fermentation.

5. Wine grapes are the number one fruit crop in the world in terms of acres planted.

6. The "right" and "wrong" way to hold a wine glass is not just myth perpetrated by wine snobs. The rational for holding the glass by the stem and not the bowl is that it avoids warming the temperature of the wine through the heat emanating from your hand. This could influence the wine's taste.

7. European wines are named after their geographic location (e.g., Burgundy, Bordeaux and Champagne). Non-European wines (e.g., Merlot) are named after different grape varieties.

BORDEAUX

🍇 Route des Vins

　　　Snob Free Wine Tasting Companion

Greeks and Romans

- The modern day ritual of drinking "to your health" hearkens back to ancient Greece. Then, the host would taste the wine before his guests to show them it was not poisoned.

- Romans dropped pieces of bread into wine glasses to offset acid or other undesirable tastes. Hence, the term "toasting" when we drink wine.

- Over the years various historians have hypothesized that lead poisoning caused the decline of Rome. In particular, because the Romans mixed lead with wine to preserve it and enhance its taste, and stored wine in lead-containing vessels, indulgence in wine drinking is cited as a contributing factor to the culture's demise. The debate remains alive today.

- We've come a long way. In early Roman times, women were forbidden to drink wine. If a husband found his wife drinking, he was permitted to divorce or even kill her! The last recorded Roman divorce on these grounds was dated in 194 B.C.

8 Champagne is often erroneously thought to have been invented by the Benedictine monk Dom Pierre Pérignon (1638-1715). No doubt the confusion arises because there is a Dom Pérignon Champagne produced by Moët & Chandon, a winery in France. Dom Pérignon did, however, create many principles and processes still used in the production of champagne today.

9 Wine jars unearthed with the Tutankhamen tomb in 1922, were labeled with the year, the name of the wine maker, and comments about the wine quality. Surprisingly, the labels were so specific they could meet today's wine label regulations in several countries!

10 In ancient Babylon, the bride's father provided his son-in-law with a month's worth of mead (a fermented honey beverage) to consume after the wedding. The Babylonian calendar was lunar-based and this period of free mead was called the "honey month". The term "honey-moon" is thought to have evolved from honey month. For newly wed gentlemen reading this book, you now have an excuse to pitch your father-in-law for a month of wine!

11 Prior to the development of cork as a bottle closure in the 17th century, bottles were short and bulbous. Once cork closures were in common use, bottle shapes slowly evolved to the tall and slender shape we know today and began to be laid down for aging.

12 It is not the case that all wines improve over time and must be aged. On the contrary, the majority of wines produced are ready to drink and are not enhanced much by aging. One can also keep a wine too long. It is rare that wine lasts beyond a decade.

13 Monastic orders were the best and most innovative wine makers in the Middle Ages. The Cistercians and Benedictines had strong reputations as wine makers, and are said to have actually tasted the soil to learn how it differed from location to location. Most growers today would probably be averse to the soil tasting technique but all would respect the recognition that soil varies and affects the wine.

14 In 79 AD, when Mount Vesuvius buried Pompeii in volcanic ash and pumice, more than 200 wine bars were also buried, to be excavated in 1748.

Gender Differences

Women's susceptibility to alcohol effects is greater than men's. In part this is due to less of an enzyme in the lining of the stomach that is needed to metabolize alcohol efficiently. Additionally, due to a lower fat to liquid ratio, alcohol goes to the brain more quickly.

Since wine tasting is essentially wine smelling, women tend to be "better" wine tasters because they have a better sense of smell than men, particularly when women are of reproductive age. This means they can pick up more nuanced flavors.

17   The Most Popular Red Wines and Food Pairings

WINE	FOOD PAIRINGS
● **Pinot Noir** (pronounced Pee´-no Na-wahr´) A very light red grape. It is described as delicate and fresh. The aroma is soft and fruity (cherry, strawberry, plum and watermelon) and may have notes of tea, damp earth, and worn leather. One of the thinnest-skinned grapes and lightest varietals.	Grilled salmon, chicken, lamb and Japanese dishes such as sushi rolls. 
● **Grenache** (pronounced Greh-nosh´) One of the most widely planted varieties in the world in Spain, Australia, Italy, France and the U.S. Aromas of strawberry, black cherry, and raspberry. Sometimes tobacco, cinnamon and citrus rind can be tasted.	Stews (pork and lamb), barbecue, turkey, paella, roasted meats. 

WINE	FOOD PAIRINGS
● **Merlot** (pronounced Mare-loh´) Merlot can be fruit forward with smooth tannins (less tannic than Cab). Typical aromas: blackberry, plums, and herbal flavors. Great beginning wine for new red wine drinkers.	Steak with sauces, casseroles, leg of lamb, roast duck, roast turkey, spaghetti, baked pasta dishes such as lasagna. 
● **Sangiovese** (pronounced San-gee-oh-ve´-zee) Sangiovese is medium-bodied and aromatic like Pinot Noir, but has bigger tannins, with cherry and plum flavors. Other subspecies or clones are → Sangiovese-pinto/Chianti → Sangiovese-grosso/Brunello	Italian dishes such as chicken parmesan, meat lasagna, sausage pizza and other dishes containing acidic tomato sauces and grilled red meat. 
● **Nebbiolo** (pronounced Neh-be-oh-lo) Grown mostly in northwest Italy, Nebbiolo is a savory high-tannin and acid wine, light in color.	Barbecue, grilled meats, beef, short ribs, pasta with red sauce, prime rib roast, game birds, chicken cacciatore.
● **Tempranillo** (pronounced Temp-ra-knee´-oh) Tempranillo is a dominant Spanish grape varietal which produces a medium-to-full-bodied wine. It has flavor characteristics of black plum, boysenberry, and strawberry. Secondary flavors of pepper and vanilla are often detected.	Roast chicken, braised lamb shank, beef short ribs, lamb chops, roast leg of lamb, rosemary steak, chicken enchiladas, grilled eggplant, hamburgers, prime rib, pizza, veal parmigiana, and seafood paella.

WINE	FOOD PAIRINGS

● Cabernet Sauvignon
(pronounced
Cab-burr-nay´ So-veen-yaw´)

One of the most balanced full-bodied wines in the world. Characterized by a long finish, full-body and high tannins, as well as rich fruit characteristics. Cabs have mutiple flavors that may include plum, cherry, blackberry, blueberry, warm spice, vanilla, tobacco and leather aromas.

Red meats, flavorful (red) pastas, lamb, strong-flavored cheese, and chocolates (especially dark, with 70% or more cacao).

● Syrah/Shiraz
(pronounced Sah-ra´ or Shi-raz´)

Syrah offers big, bold, dark fruit flavors upfront with a subtle finish and lighter tannin. Flavors from olive to blackberry and tobacco.

Meat, beef, steak and wild game.

● Malbec
(pronounced Mal´-bek)

Malbec is a medium-to-full-bodied wine with fruit flavors of plums, black cherry and blackberry. Also characterized by a jammy character, sometimes with aromas of smoke, leather, tobacco, and black pepper.

Spicy barbecue sauces with lamb, beef, or pork, meat dishes, spaghetti and meatballs, burgers, roast beef, fajitas, duck, lamb curry.

18 The Most Popular White Wines and Food Pairings

WINE	FOOD PAIRINGS
Pinot Grigio (pronounced Pee´-no Gree´-zio) Crisp (high acid) dry wine typically made in U.S. Western coastal regions, Italy, Loire Valley of France and Germany. Flavors found in Pinot Grigio can be melon, pear, citrus fruits, and tropical fruits. Honey and smoky flavors may be tasted.	Pastas, seafood, variety of cheeses. Avoid food pairing with high acid contents like tomato recipes or citrus fruits. 
Riesling (pronounced Rees´-ling) Dry-to-sweet white Rieslings have an aroma of fresh apples, lime, honey and apricots with high acidity.	Dry Rieslings pair well with fish, chicken and pork dishes. Japanese dishes work well with Rieslings. Halibut with orange sauce, bacon and egg pizza, honey soy roasted pork, sheep cheese soufflé, Thai ground pork salad, ham and gruyère, French toast sandwiches, stir fry shrimp with bacon, mint and chiles.

WINE	FOOD PAIRINGS
○ **Sauvignon Blanc** (pronounced So-veen-yawn´ Blah´) Typical taste in this varietal is bell pepper, freshly mown grass, with flavors of sour green fruits like apples and pears. Other flavors tasted are tropical fruits of melon, mango, papaya, and citrus fruits such as grapefruit.	Seafood, poultry, and salads. 
○ **Chenin Blanc** (pronounced Shen´-in Blah´) Produced in dry, off-dry and sweet styles. Characterized by flavors of melon, pear, apricots, nectarine, citrus, and green apple.	Crab, roast duck, Japanese cuisine, Chinese egg rolls, spinach dip, barbecue pork, barbecue chicken, chicken soup, Camembert cheese, ham with pineapple, cream soups, potato soup. Sweet Chenin Blanc pairs well with peach cobbler, apricot tarts and apple desserts. 
○ **Moscato** (pronounced Mos-ca´to) Sweet dessert wine with fruity tastes like peaches and orange blossom. The dry version of the Muscat grape is found all over the world in different types, as well as a sparkling version in Italy.	On its own as a dessert wine. The dry Muscat will pair with dark fish, curry, Indian cuisine, and spicy dishes. 

WINE	FOOD PAIRINGS
○ Gewürztraminer (pronounced Gah-vurtz-tra-meen´er) Ranges from "off-dry" to sweet white wines that taste of fruity flavors, ginger and honey. Aromas of peaches, rose petals and allspice may be detected.	Asian food, pork, and grilled sausages. 
○ Sémillon (pronounced Seh-me-yohn´) Dry medium-bodied wines with lemon notes and fig character. Often blended with other white wines.	Light fish, shrimp, clams, mussels, Japanese cuisine, and pasta salad. 
○ Viognier (pronounced Vee-oh-nyay´) Medium-bodied white wines that smell like flowers.	Pork, seafood such as halibut, Thai salads, chicken tetrazzini, pasta primavera, seafood chowder, Mexican dip with nachos, lamb curry, lobster bisque, white clam chowder, chicken marsala, sushi, roast turkey, pasta with seafood sauce, and spinach dip. Light foods will be overpowered by Viognier. 

○ **Chardonnay**
   (pronounced Shar-doh-nay´)

The most popular white wine grape originating from the Burgundy region, Bourgogne, France. Chardonnay makes great sparkling wine grown in cooler regions. Typical tastes are of citrus, lemon and grapefruit flavors. When fermented in oak barrels and put through secondary fermentation (malolactic), Chardonnay will taste buttery and often of vanilla, toast, coconut and toffee.

Fish (especially salmon) and chicken dishes, roast chicken, salmon with cream sauces, frittatas, salads, crab cakes, chicken dijon, oysters, pork with cream sauce, shrimp with cream sauce.

19   Wine and Cheese Pairing Guide

If you're planning a picnic in the wine country, cheese and wine make great partners. Impress your friends at home too by pairing wines and cheeses at a party. When paired, wine and food have a "synergy," or an additional flavor, beyond what either offers alone.

The saying goes, "The sweeter the wine, the stronger the cheese." The following chart can help you decide what cheeses to serve with different types of wine. You can find much longer lists of wine and cheese pairings, however, in keeping with the Snob Free theme, this is designed to get you started with generally well-known cheeses with which you may already be familiar. As is always the case, only you can decide what tastes good to you.

KIND OF WINE	BEST PAIRED WITH
○ White Wines	**Soft cheeses** Stronger flavors, such as: brie, goat cheese, gruyère, parmesan, jarlsberg
● Red Wines	**Hard cheeses** Milder flavors, such as: sharp cheddar, gouda, Danish blue, edam, gruyère, brie
Fruity, Sweet Dessert Wines, Sherry and Port	**A wide range of cheeses** Stronger flavors, such as: strong blue cheeses, gorgonzola, stilton

20 Pairing Wine with Chocolate

O kay. We have arrived at what I consider a gustatory delight: wine and chocolate. It's hard to go wrong when wine and chocolate are paired together; there is a surprising synergy that makes you want to keep experimenting. If it weren't for the calories, this would be a staple in my diet. Julia Child provides me encouragement, though, to put the calorie counter away: "Everything in moderation, including moderation." Here are a few methods to help you get started on your chocolate and wine pairing, when you want to indulge:

1 **Follow the first rule of pairing food and wine.**
The chocolate should not be sweeter than the wine you are pairing it with. Take a little taste of chocolate before you pair with the wine.

2 **Purchase high-quality chocolate for the purpose of pairing wine with chocolate.**
Examples are: Lindt, Ghirardelli, Godiva, Scharffen Berger, or Guittard, whether white, dark or milk chocolate.

3 **Pair chocolate and wine consistent with the darkness of the chocolate.**
As a general rule the darker the wine, the darker the chocolate you should select. Red wines pair best with dark chocolate.

4 **Locate wines that are not highly astringent to pair with chocolate.**
Wines with smooth texture are important when pairing with chocolate. See the chart.

5 **Match full-bodied wines to strong, intense, and heavy chocolates.**
See the chart.

6 Move from light to dark chocolate if trying more than one pairing.
Begin with light milk and white chocolates, move on to more medium intensities and culminate your wine and chocolate tasting with dark chocolate.

7 Experiment with many combinations.
The following chart contains only guidelines from which to start experimenting. The adventure is to find the matches that suit your own taste.

CHOCOLATE TYPE	WINE SUGGESTIONS
White Chocolate	Sweet, Sparkling Chardonnay Riesling
Milk Chocolate	Pinot Noir Light Merlot Riesling Tawny Port Muscat
Raisinettes Work well from the synergy of grapes and chocolate. Have fun!	Big, bold red wines
Dark Chocolate (50% to 70% cacao content or higher; stronger intensity chocolate goes with stronger flavored wines)	Zinfandel Merlot Syrah/Shiraz Cabernet Sauvignon Tawny Port Cognac

21 Important Facts about Napa Valley

1 4% of the wine produced in California comes from Napa Valley.

2 9% of Napa County land is planted with wine grapes.

3 Napa Valley is 16% the size of Bordeaux, France.

4 Napa Valley has a Mediterranean climate that is found in only about 2% of the Earth's surface. Long, warm summer days and appreciably cooler nights are optimal for growing wine grapes.

5 The topography includes narrow, linear valleys; steep mountain slopes and ridges; high plateaus and a flat valley floor along with low, sloping alluvial fans.

6 Soil in Napa Valley is extremely varied; half of the world's soil types can be found here in an area only 30 miles long and one to five miles wide. There are over 40 different soil types in Napa Valley. The most common are: alluvial, volcanic, and sedimentary.

- **Alluvial Soil:** Deposited by ancient river flows; this soil is cobbly, stony, gravelly and excessively drained with moderate-to-low nutrient content. Cabernet Sauvignon grown in this type of soil may develop flavors that are earthy, aromatic, complex, and concentrated.

- **Volcanic Soil:** Formed by local volcanic flows of lava and ash. This soil is poor in nutrient and organic material and excessively-to-well-drained. Cabernet Sauvignon grown in this type of soil may develop flavors that are spicy, cedary, and often minty.

- **Sedimentary Soil:** Richer loamy soils formed by the settling of an ancient sea or lake, these can be poorly drained and have good nutrient and organic composition. Cabernet Sauvignon grown in this type of soil may develop flavors that are fruity and can be herbal and strongly flavored.

7 The elevation of Napa Valley ranges from sea level to 2,600 feet above sea level.

8 There are 16 approved sub-appellations in the Napa Valley American Viticultural Area (AVA), each with its own recognized unique climate, and soil characteristics, known as terroir.

9 Produces more than three dozen varieties of wine grapes.

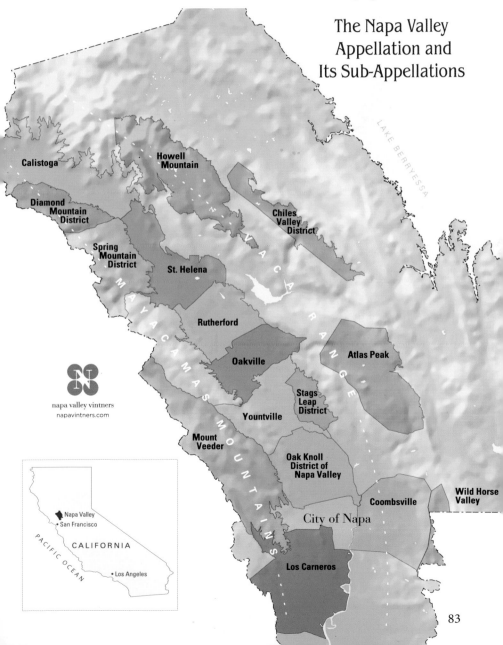

The Napa Valley Appellation and Its Sub-Appellations

Calistoga

Howell Mountain

Diamond Mountain District

Chiles Valley District

Spring Mountain District

St. Helena

Rutherford

Atlas Peak

Oakville

Stags Leap District

Yountville

Mount Veeder

Oak Knoll District of Napa Valley

Coombsville

Wild Horse Valley

City of Napa

Los Carneros

LAKE BERRYESSA

MAYACAMAS RANGE

MOUNTAINS

napa valley vintners
napavintners.com

Napa Valley
San Francisco
CALIFORNIA
Los Angeles
PACIFIC OCEAN

22 Important Facts about Sonoma County

- Sonoma County is 21% the size of Bordeaux, France.
- The long, dry, sunny summer days with cool nights, ocean breezes and fog, produce the optimal conditions for growing wine grapes.
- Sonoma County is a million acres (1,604 square miles) of valley floors, rolling hills and tree-lined mountainsides.
- Sonoma County has more soil types than France, ranging from rich and loamy to volcanic and well-drained.
- It is the birthplace of the California wine industry, with several generations of families devoted to its land for their livelihood.
- Producing more than 66 varieties of wine grapes, Sonoma County is the most diverse premium wine grape-growing region in the United States. Seven varieties comprise nearly 94% of the tons of grapes crushed in Sonoma County:
  - Chardonnay (America's most popular white wine): 16,000 acres
  - Sauvignon Blanc: 2,500 acres
  - Cabernet Sauvignon: 12,000 acres
  - Merlot: 7,500 acres
  - Pinot Noir: 10,000 acres
  - Zinfandel: 5,000 acres
  - Syrah: 1,820 acres

Mendocino County

Annapolis

Pacific Ocean

SONOMA COUNTY

San Francisco

www.sonomawine.com

- Countywide, the annual production of table, sparkling and dessert wines is estimated at more than 30 million gallons, from approximately 200,000 tons of grapes.

- Sonoma County has several wine regions worth visiting:

  - Sonoma Valley
  - Russian River Valley
  - Dry Creek Valley
  - Alexander Valley
  - Los Carneros
  - Moon Mountain
  - Sonoma Mountain
  - Bennett Valley
  - Green Valley
  - Knights Valley
  - Rockpile
  - Sonoma Coast
  - Chalk Hill
  - Fort Ross-Seaview
  - Pine Mountain-Cloverdale Park

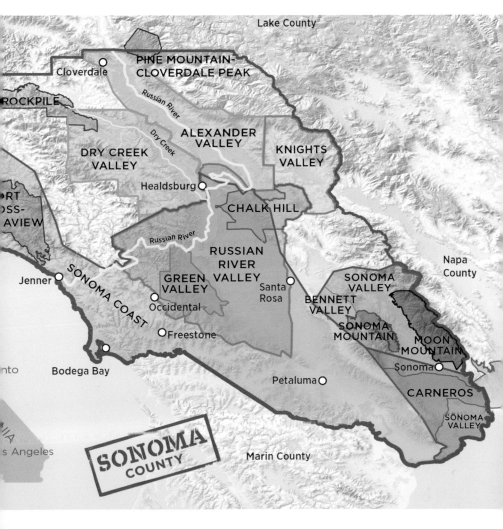

23   Historical Highlights of Napa and Sonoma Wine Country

Russian Colonies Plant Grapes — 1732 to 1867

Russian colonists searching beyond Russia for fur-bearing mammals laid claim to the Pacific Coast territories in the Americas in the 1700s and 1800s. Wine grapes were planted by Russian colonists at Fort Ross on the Sonoma coast as early as 1812.

Mid-19th century — Russia's American colonies were in decline. The population of fur-bearing mammals was on the wane and the sea otter was near extinction. Faced with periodic Indian revolts, the Russians were unable to colonize America to their satisfaction. They sold Fort Ross in Sonoma County and soon after 1867, sold Alaska to the U.S. for $7.2 million. This ended Russia's colonial presence in the Americas.

The Mission Period — 1769 to 1833

Spanish Catholics of the Franciscan Order established Spanish missions in California as religious and military outposts to spread Christianity. California had several native grapes growing along the rivers in the valleys, but they were not suited for wine making. The minor Spanish grape variety called the Listan Prieto was planted at all mission pueblos and ranchos except San Francisco and Santa Cruz, where it was too cold. These grapes were used primarily for sacramental purposes. The last of the 21 California missions was San Francisco de Solano, founded in 1823 in the town of Sonoma.

Mariano Guadalupe Vallejo, Commander of the Sonoma Pueblo

Quick Facts:

- Assumed the position of Military Governor of Mexican California until the Bear Flag Revolt of 1846; a small group of American settlers rebelled against the Mexican government, and proclaimed California an independent republic. The republic lasted a matter of days at which point the U.S. military began occupying the area. California went on to join the union in 1850.

- Built the Sonoma Barracks at the northeast corner of the Sonoma town square to protect Mexico's interest in the area. The barracks are still standing.

- Replanted the Sonoma Mission; plant cuttings from Sonoma were distributed throughout northern California to start new vineyards.

- Became the first grower of wine grapes outside of the missions and won gold medals at the State Fair of 1858.

- Inspired many to settle on the north coast, including George Yount and Charles Krug.

Gold Rush of 1849

The epicenter of the Gold Rush was approximately 60 miles east of Napa Valley, just northeast of Sacramento, in the foothills of the Sierra Nevada Mountains. Not only were Americans drawn to the area, people from all parts of the world were lured by tales of gold. Before 1850, the main crops in the Napa Valley area involved fields of wheat, walnut trees, fruit tree orchards and prunes. The Gold Rush directly impacted the development of the wine country in Napa and Sonoma:

- The Gold Rush created a new market for wine, fresh fruit and nuts.

- The Gold Rush brought more experienced wine makers to California from Europe.

- Charles Kohler and John Frohling built a large winery on Sonoma Mountain and planted 350 acres. Through an agency in New York they distributed wine nationwide.

Some settlers in Napa and Sonoma who came from Europe brought with them family vineyard experience going back centuries. They planted the first vines in Napa and Sonoma in the 1850s, with the expectation that grapes would grow as well here as in Europe. Unfortunately, the wine they produced was not considered good. The early settlers did, however, leave a legacy: they got the wine industry started in the Napa and Sonoma region.

Agoston Haraszthy, [Ha ra´ zee]
Founder of Buena Vista Winery

- Energetic entrepreneur from Hungary who wanted to grow wine grapes.
- Traveled from Wisconsin to San Diego by wagon train in 1849.
- First Sheriff of Middle Town near San Diego.
- Elected to California State Legislature.
- Grew grapes in Santa Clara.
- In 1857 bought vineyards in Sonoma and founded Buena Vista Winery, first commercial winery in California.

- Promoted California wine making and founded a California Viticultural Society.

- 1861 — Went to Europe and brought back 100,000 European varietal grape cuttings, and better techniques for wine making.

- Published a pamphlet on wine making, which established him as the father of California viticulture.

- Buena Vista grew to production of one million wine cases per year by 1873.

Snob Free Wine Tasting Companion

- 1866 — Agoston Haraszthy left for Nicaragua. The quality of Sonoma's wine industry increased through the shake-out of poor wine making practices.
- It cost more to pick grapes than the wine was worth after fermentation.
- Wineries such as Gundlach Bundschu, Foppiano, Korbel, Simi, Quitzow, Kunde and Sebastiani became established and have survived well into the twenty-first century.

1850 to 1900

Phylloxera, a tiny aphid-like insect, created serious damage in California and European vineyards

- Introduced to Europe by a few English botanists who brought home American vines in the 1850s, the pest devastated over 70% of the European wine industry, mostly in France.
- First spotted in California in 1873.

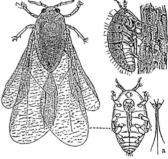

- Ignored in Sonoma until becoming a serious problem.
- George Husmann and Eugene Hilgard credited with experimenting with planting of Phylloxera-resistent rootstock.
- Solution was to graft European varieties on American rootstock, which was more resistant.

Wine Quality Boost by Two Notables

George de Latour

Though earlier European Gold Rush settlers could not grow good quality wine, in the early 1900s two big names turned the tide. The first was a Frenchman named George de Latour. He came to the Napa Valley and brought with him over 100,000 cuttings of vines from France, giving the cuttings to anyone who wanted to plant them. This contributed to a renewed focus on grape growing in Napa. George de Latour founded the now-famous BV winery: Beaulieu Vineyards.

André Tchelistcheff [chill-ist-chef]

In search of a new wine maker with a scientific background, de Latour visited France and found the experience he was looking for in the famous wine maker, André Tchelistcheff.

In 1938 Tchelistcheff became BV's Vice President and chief wine maker. Tchelistcheff's impact at BV and in the region was profound. He defined a style for high-quality Cabernet Sauvignon, and created the "George de Latour Private Reserve" label. He introduced new French techniques to the region, including aging wine in small French oak barrels. By the mid-1940s, "Private Reserve" was widely recognized as the gold standard for California Cabernet Sauvignon, and was even served at White House functions.

American oak barrel storage took place after the United States entered World War II and became an accepted tradition at BV under Tchelistcheff and his successors. Tchelistcheff made significant contributions to the techniques of cold soaking fermentation, frost protection during bud break in the vineyard, and malolactic fermentation. His mark was far reaching and included the development of wine making regions in Napa Valley, Sonoma County and the states of Oregon and Washington. He was widely responsible for improving the quality of Napa wines.

1920 to 1933: Prohibition

- January 16, 1920 — The 18th Amendment, the Volstead Act, goes into effect, banning the manufacture, sale and transport of alcoholic beverages.

- The wine industry attempts unsuccessfully to keep wine separate from distilled spirits.

- Napa and Sonoma winery closures: before Prohibition, Sonoma had 256 wineries; after Prohibition, less than 50 wineries remain in Sonoma, and most in Napa are closed.

- The Foppiano Winery in Sonoma County is forced to dump its wine into a creek.

- In spite of Prohibition:
  - The church could make sacramental wine.
  - Anxious individuals could get a prescription to drink wine for anxiety.
  - Those establishments that survived Prohibition produce sacramental wine and medicated "wine tonics." (Some were involved in bootlegging.)

- The Volstead Act allows individuals to produce up to 200 gallons of wine per year for personal use; people make "non-intoxicating fruit beverages or cider" in their homes.

Can't buy wine? Make it at home!

Prior to the Golden Gate Bridge completion in 1937, there were no bridges over the San Francisco Bay. Only ferries carried people from San Francisco to other destinations in the vicinity. During Prohibition, people would ferry across the bay to Marin County, then board a train to Calistoga in Napa Valley, or stop at the small town of Sonoma. Their trips would include stays at hotels, and bed and breakfast inns. Prior to their return to the city, they would buy grapes to take back to San Francisco from farmers who stood along the train tracks. Thus San Franciscans got supplies to make wine in their basements and bathtubs. Where there's a will, there's a way!

- Because of Prohibition, demand for varietal juice grapes goes from $10 per ton in 1918 to $100 per ton in 1920.

- People get used to mediocre homemade wine.

- Prohibition leads to organized crime and loss of tax revenues.

- December 5, 1933 — The Repeal of the Volstead Act. Alcohol production and consumption becomes more regulated. Every state makes its own laws; variable state regulations still exist today.

Mid 1930s to 1960s

* During World War II, G.I.'s are introduced in Europe to quality table wine for the first time.
* Also, during World War II, importing of European wines ceases and demand for domestic wine increases.
* Cheap jug and flavored wines dominate, e.g. Thunderbird, Mad Dog 20/20, Boone's Farm, Ripple.
* The number one wine in the 1960s is Cream Sherry.
* In 1966 there are 231 wineries in all of California (18 in Sonoma and 15 in Napa).
* 1968: Dry wine outsells sweet wine for the first time since Prohibition.

The 1970s: A Wine Revolution

* Early 1970s wine consumption grows by 40%.
* Wine labels are regulated and wine appellations become important in marketing.
* 1976: Sonoma County has 24,000 acres of grapes (twice the acreage of 10 years before).

The New Pioneers of Wine Making

* Wineries began using malolactic fermentation, French oak barrels, and stainless steel tanks, which were temperature-controlled, as well as nitrogen gas to prevent oxidation.

The new generation of wine makers in the 1970s included:

* Robert Mondavi of Robert Mondavi Winery
* Jack and Jamie Davies of Schramsberg
* Warren Winiarski of Stags' Leap Wine Cellars
* Jim Barrett of Chateau Montelena
* The Lee Family of Kenwood Vineyards
* These pioneers had a passion for making world-class wine!

Robert Mondavi changes everything...

Robert Mondavi is considered the visionary behind a shift in Napa Valley to world-class wine making in the last half of the twentieth century.

Emigrating from Italy, Robert's family settled in Minnesota, where Robert was born. The family later moved to Lodi, a little town 1½ hours east of Napa. There, Robert's father, Cesare, established a successful fruit-packing and shipping business, sending California varietal grapes to East Coast wineries. The business launched under the name C. Mondavi and Sons.

Robert went to Stanford University, where he received a degree in business and economics. After he graduated, he came back to join the family business, working with his father and his brother Peter.

Sensing a good business opportunity, Robert persuaded his father to come over to the Napa Valley to the St. Helena area and purchase an historic winery built in 1861: the Charles Krug Winery. The Mondavi family operated it as their business for many years, improving the quality of wine produced there. However, more improvements and changes were to come.

1959 — Cesare Mondavi died, leaving the running of the winery to his two sons, Robert and Peter.

1965 — Robert separated from the Charles Krug Winery over disputes with his brother about the best approach to wine production. Robert was convinced that world-class wine could not be produced in the style then used by the Charles Krug Winery and was determined to test other approaches.

1966 — Robert opened the Robert Mondavi Winery. From the 1930s to the 1960s, Napa Valley had been a sleepy place. This was the first new winery built in over 30 years.

Robert went to France to learn the French approach to wine making.

He brought back small 60-gallon French oak barrels for use in his Napa Valley winery, then began using "cold soaking fermentation" and other techniques. Overwhelmingly, Robert Mondavi was becoming known for something different in wine making.

Robert Mondavi changes the wine culture from competitive to collaborative:

Most business people are interested in keeping a distance between themselves and their competitors. But Robert Mondavi was the exact opposite. He had a burning passion to bring various winery businesses together as a group to collaborate in making great wine.

He facilitated this by opening up his new winery once a week, inviting wine makers to meet and share their wine making techniques. All the Napa Valley wineries joined in. Wine making became a group effort there. If a wine maker was sick or injured, another wine maker would provide help. If equipment broke down at one winery, another wine maker would loan his winery's equipment. If one winery had a labor shortage at harvest time, another winery would lend its labor.

Such remarkable cooperation greatly accelerated the learning curve of all the wine makers. In a few years, Napa Valley created an explosion of world-class wines.

Robert Mondavi died in 2009 at age 94, leaving behind a dramatic legacy in wine quality, wine production processes and the cooperative approach to wine making he had established in Napa. He became renowned not only in the United States, but internationally as well.

1976: The "Judgment of Paris"

France was known throughout the world as having the best quality wine; Napa wines, though becoming better known, were not yet viewed in the same league as French wines. Steven Spurrier, a prominent Paris wine merchant and wine educator, had a goal of creating publicity for himself. He established a wine tasting contest: a blind taste test of France's best wines and Napa Valley's best wines.

Contest Rules

1 The contest had to be held in Paris, France, at the Intercontinental Hotel.

2 Both Napa and France had to come up with their very best white and red wines for the contest.

3 When the bottles were poured, they had to be wrapped in paper bags so the judges would have a "blind" tasting.

4 All nine judges had to be renowned French experts in the world of fine wine.

Shockingly, most of the contest winners turned out to be Napa wines, as judged by the nine French experts! The top red wine and three of the top four whites, including the first-place winner, were produced in Napa Valley vineyards.

George Tabor, an international journalist, was asked to cover the contest. His article appeared in *Time* magazine: "Judgment of Paris: Napa Wines Judged Best in the World by the French Themselves." To the chagrin of the French wine industry, California wine was propelled onto the world stage through that article, describing quality that not only met French standards, but exceeded them.

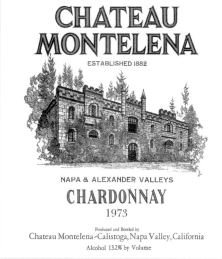

In 1976, the California legislature passed a bill proclaiming the Judgment of Paris an historical event. A bottle of each of the first-place wines was placed in a permanent exhibit at the Smithsonian:

- Chateau Montelena Chardonnay
- Stags' Leap Wine Cellars Cabernet Sauvignon

Bottle Shock, a movie about the Judgment of Paris, premiered at the 2008 Sundance Festival.

The impact of the Judgment of Paris included an explosion of free publicity that was showered upon Napa Valley. It was now validated beyond any further debate that Napa was a world-class wine region. California's wine country saw a dramatic increase in interest; investment in and development of land and vineyards escalated at a frenzied pace. There were 60+ wineries in the late 1970s in the Napa Valley; today, there are over 475 wineries in Napa and over 400 wineries in Sonoma.

1980s

- Sonoma County transitions its agricultural production from a focus on dairy, grain and fruit crops to wine grapes, which become its top revenue-generating crop.

- Phylloxera becomes a problem again; shows up in a new form.
- Many vineyards are replanted with better clones.
- The new vineyards are vastly improved, at great expense.
- In 1989, there are 771 wineries in California.

1990s

- People drinking less wine, but better quality.
- Wine still considered a luxury product.
- New information about drinking wine in moderation being good for your health boosts wine sales.
- In Sonoma County, more vineyard acreage comes at expense of other crops.
- 73% of Sonoma County agricultural production is involved in growing wine grapes; over 1,100 growers here.
- By 1999, there are 1,200 wineries in California.

2001 to 2008

- Boom of higher grape prices and overplanting in 1990s leads to a surplus of grapes.
- Weaker dollar makes imported wine more expensive; exports from California become cheaper.
- Economic recession impacts wineries hard.
- Expensive wine sales decrease, while less expensive wines increase in sales.
- Consumers seek value instead of prestige.

The future of wine in California

- Entering the "Golden Age of Wine" for the consumer, with more value and choice.
- Consolidation of small- and mid-sized wineries is likely to continue.
- Urban growth pressure on agricultural land will continue.
- Climate change will impact agricultural products.

24   Quick Wine Glossary

Acidity: A natural component in grapes that gives the wine a snappy, refreshing taste. Wines with very little acid are characterized as "dull," "flabby," "unfocused." Wines with too much acidity taste tart. A wine balanced in acidity will taste "crisp."

Appellation/Viticultural Area/AVA: Defines a legal grape-growing area with specific climate, soil, elevation and history (terroir). A wine must be made with at least 85% of grapes from a specific AVA to be labeled with that appellation.

Barrel-Fermented: Wine fermented in 60-gallon oak barrels instead of larger steel tanks. Oak barrels increase body and add flavor, texture, and complexity to the wine.

Body: The sensation of the wine's weight in your mouth. It is usually described as light-, medium-, or full-bodied, as in the case of heavier wines like Cabernet Sauvignon. This is related to the total amount of fruit, alcohol, and tannin in the wine.

Brix: Measurement of sugar content in grapes. Brix indicates the degree of ripeness at harvest. Most grapes are harvested between 22 and 27 Brix, with a late harvest dessert wine at 30 Brix or more.

Decant: A process of slowly pouring wines into a carafe to leave the wine's sediment behind and to expose the wine to air for the purpose of releasing its bouquet.

Estate: A term used to indicate that the wine was produced from grapes grown on winery-owned or leased land, and that the winery had control of the wine-making process from grape-growing to finished bottling.

Fermentation: The process that turns grape juice into wine: yeast converts sugar to alcohol and carbon dioxide.

Filtering: The process of removing particles from wine after fermentation. Filtering adds clarity to the wine. Some small wineries prefer not to filter their wine.

Finish: The length of time flavors linger in the mouth after the wine has been swallowed. Excellent wines have long, complex finishes. A major key to judging a wine's quality, finish is also referred to as the "aftertaste."

Flabby: Lacking in acidity.

Fortified Wine: A wine whose alcohol content has been increased by adding brandy, grappa, or neutral 100% alcohol to make Port or Sherry.

Free-Run Juice: Free-run juice is the liquid that is produced by the natural breakdown of the grape cell wall, due to the weight of the grape berries as they are loaded into the press. About 60%-70% of the available liquid within the grape berry, the free-run juice, will be released by this process alone and does not require the actual use of the press.

Maceration: "Must" (the grape skins and solids) is mixed with the grape juice liquid for the purpose of extracting color, tannin and aroma from the skins. This occurs during the fermentation process.

Malolactic Fermentation: A process that happens naturally or may be induced, where a beneficial bacteria converts malic acid (very tart) in wine to lactic acid, to produce a softer flavor in the wine. It adds complexity to wines such as Chardonnay and softens red wines such as Merlot and Cabernet Sauvignon.

Non-Vintage: A wine blended from more than one growing season. This allows a winery to produce a "house blend."

Oxidized: A wine that has been exposed to air too long and has typically turned brown. It loses its freshness and begins to smell like old apples. Also referred to as "maderized."

Residual Sugar: Unfermented grape sugar in a finished wine bottle.

Sulfites/Sulfur: Sulfur is used in wine and vineyards to preserve and protect grapes from unwanted bacteria. Sulfites occur naturally as a byproduct of fermentation, or may be added by the wine maker.

Labeling laws require a winery to state the parts per million (ppm) of sulfites contained in each bottle.

Tart: A sharp-tasting wine whose taste is caused by acidity.

Tartaric Acid: The principal acid contained in wine.

Tawny: Refers to a sweet or medium dry Port, lighter in color and body than a "ruby" Port. Usually aged from ten to thirty years.

Vintage Date: Indicates the year that the grapes were picked and the wine was made. Ninety-five percent of the grapes in a given bottle must come from the year stated to justify the vintage date on the bottle.

Viticultural Area (AVA): See Appellation.

25 References

82 Delicious Facts about Wine — Random History. (n.d.). Retrieved from http://facts.randomhistory.com/2009/08/21_wine.html

Bear Flag Revolt — Facts & Summary-HISTORY.com. (n.d.). Retrieved from http://www.history.com/topics/bear-flag-revolt

Boisset Collection, Boisset Family Estates, Buena Vista Winery

Choosing Wines to Pair with Dark Chocolates — Wine.Answers.com (n.d.). Retrieved from http://wine.answeres.com/types-of-wine/chosing-wines-to-pari-with-dark-chocolates

Corked, Cooked, Bretty, Bad: How to Spot 7 Common Wine Flaws… (n.d.) Retrieved from http://drinks.seriouseats.com/2013/09/how-to-identify-if-your-wine-is-off-corked-cooked-va-brett-wine-flaws.html

Constellation Brands, Inc., Robert Mondavi winery

COUNSIL DECISION on the conclusion of the Agreement between …(n.d.). Retrieved from http://www.europarl.europa.eu/meet-docs/2009_2004/document

Defining 18 Noble Grapes to Expand Your Palate I Wine Folly. (n.d.). Retrieved from http://winefolly.com/update/the-18-grapes-wine-challenge/

Delicious Facts About..Wine. (n.d.). Retrieved from http://www.golocal-tours.com.au/i/dleicious-facts-about-wine/

"Did you know that | Wine Story. (n.d.) Retrieved from http://www.winestory.ro/en/stiati-ca/

Does Vine Age Matter? I Napa Valley Wine Tasting Articles, http://www.cask23.com/collectorsCorner/article/27

French vs. American Oak I Jade Ranch Wine. (n.d.). Retrieved from http://www.jaderanchwine.com/the-barn-french-vs-american-oak/

Fun facts about wine I TheHill – The Hill – covering Congress…(n.d.) Retrieved from http://thehill.com/capital-living/vino-veritas/313341-fun-facs-about-wine

Main Navigation. (n.d.). Retrieved from http://www.thebestwinery.com/

My Wine Tutor: Wine Tasting Basics. (n.d.). Retrieved from http://www.mywinetutor.com/winetasting basics.html

http://www.Napavintners.com

Sbrocco, Leslie. 2003. Wine for Women: A Guide to Buying, Pairing, and Sharing Wine. New York, NY: HarperCollins.

Talk Tight, Get Heavy: How to speak wine-geek Taylor Eason…(n.d.). Retrieved from http://www/tayloreason.come/corkscrew/archives/talk-tight-get-heavy-how - to-speak-wine-geek/

http://www.Sonomawine.com

Sonoma — Wine Country Travel Guide I Winerist – Winerist. (n.d.). Retrieved from http://www.winerist.com/regions/region/sonoma

Sonoma Wine I Sonoma Wines — Wine Country Tour. (n.d.). Retrieved from http://winesounty-tour.com/sonoma-wine.html

http://www.tifachocolate.com

Toast I Seguin Moreau Napa Cooperage. (n.d.). Retrieved from http://seguinmoreaunapa.com/products/barrels/toast/

USA Wine Label Information — WineSearcher, (n.d.). Retrieved from http://www.wine-searcher.com/wine-label-usa.lml

U.S. Department of Health and Human Services, National Institutes of Health, National Institute on Alcohol and Alcoholism, NIH, Publication No. 03-4956, Revised 2008.

What are Tannins in Wine? I Wine Folly.(n.d.), Retrieved from http://winefolly.com/review/what-are-tannins-in-wine?

Wine 3 Class details & Syllabus Introduction to Enology. (n.d.). Retrieved from http://www.santarosa.edu/~jhenderson/Introduction.pdf

Wine 101 — Stemware — AgentZ. (n.d.). Retrieved from http://www.agentz.com/Wine%20101/Wine%20101%20-%20Stemware.html

Wine Facts — Questions about Wine — Delish.com (n.d.) Retrieved from http://www.delish.com/recipes/wine-guide/wine-facts

Wine facts. (n.d.). Retrieved from http://www.800wine.com/winefacts.cfm

Wine FAQ: Why Does My Wine Taste Buttery? — The Wine Feed… (n.d.). Retrieved from https://thewinefeed.com/2013/04/wine-faq-why-does-my-wine-taste-buttery/

Wine and grapes I Sonoma County Winegrowers. (n.d.). Retrieved from http://www.sonomawinegrape.org/grapes-and-wines

Wine — SCIENCE OF FOOD ENGINEERING — Google Sites. (n.d.). Retrieved from http://sites.googl.com/site/mutludemirel/food-fermentation-technology/wine

Wine Terms to Know — uvwinesandvines.(n.d.). Retrieved from http://www.uvwines.com/Wine_Terms_To_Know.html)(accessed

Wine: So what does "Fruit Forward" mean anyways…(n.d.) Retrieved from http://metrogourmand.wordpress.com/2010/01/14/wine-so-what-does-fruit-forward-mean-anyways/

Wine Words: Texture I The Kitchn. (n.d.). Retrieved from http://www.thekitchn.com/wine-words-texture-168152

Wine Tasting Notes

Vintage:	Varietal or Blend Name:
Winery:	Region:

AROMA	Aroma/Bouquet Intensity: Low Medium High
	Fruity: Green Ripe Fresh Cooked Dried Tree Fruit Citrus Tropical Berries/Cherries
	Flowery Earthy Woody Spicy Other:
TASTE	Taste/Body: Light Medium Full Sharp Mellow/Smooth
	Acidity: Low Balanced High
	Tannins: Missing Pleasing Astringent
	Finish: Short Medium Long
	My Rating: 1 2 3 4 5

Wine Tasting Notes

Vintage:	Varietal or Blend Name:
Winery:	Region:

AROMA	Aroma/Bouquet Intensity: Low Medium High
	Fruity: Green Ripe Fresh Cooked Dried Tree Fruit Citrus Tropical Berries/Cherries
	Flowery Earthy Woody Spicy Other:
TASTE	Taste/Body: Light Medium Full Sharp Mellow/Smooth
	Acidity: Low Balanced High
	Tannins: Missing Pleasing Astringent
	Finish: Short Medium Long
	My Rating: 1 2 3 4 5

Wine Tasting Notes

Vintage:	Varietal or Blend Name:	
Winery:	Region:	

AROMA

Aroma/Bouquet Intensity: Low   Medium   High

Fruity: Green   Ripe   Fresh   Cooked   Dried
Tree Fruit   Citrus   Tropical Berries/Cherries

Flowery   Earthy   Woody   Spicy   Other:

TASTE

Taste/Body: Light Medium Full Sharp Mellow/Smooth

Acidity: Low   Balanced   High

Tannins: Missing   Pleasing   Astringent

Finish: Short   Medium   Long

My Rating: 1   2   3   4   5

Wine Tasting Notes

Vintage:	Varietal or Blend Name:	
Winery:	Region:	

AROMA

Aroma/Bouquet Intensity: Low   Medium   High

Fruity: Green   Ripe   Fresh   Cooked   Dried
Tree Fruit   Citrus   Tropical Berries/Cherries

Flowery   Earthy   Woody   Spicy   Other:

TASTE

Taste/Body: Light Medium Full Sharp Mellow/Smooth

Acidity: Low   Balanced   High

Tannins: Missing   Pleasing   Astringent

Finish: Short   Medium   Long

My Rating: 1   2   3   4   5

Wine Tasting Notes

Vintage:	Varietal or Blend Name:
Winery:	Region:

<table>
<tr><td rowspan="4">A R O M A</td><td colspan="5">Aroma/Bouquet Intensity: Low   Medium   High</td></tr>
<tr><td colspan="5">Fruity: Green   Ripe   Fresh   Cooked   Dried
         Tree Fruit   Citrus   Tropical Berries/Cherries</td></tr>
<tr><td colspan="5">Flowery   Earthy   Woody   Spicy   Other:</td></tr>
</table>

TASTE	Taste/Body: Light Medium Full Sharp Mellow/Smooth
	Acidity: Low Balanced High
	Tannins: Missing Pleasing Astringent
	Finish: Short Medium Long

My Rating: 1   2   3   4   5

Wine Tasting Notes

Vintage:	Varietal or Blend Name:
Winery:	Region:

<table>
<tr><td rowspan="4">A R O M A</td><td colspan="5">Aroma/Bouquet Intensity: Low   Medium   High</td></tr>
<tr><td colspan="5">Fruity: Green   Ripe   Fresh   Cooked   Dried
         Tree Fruit   Citrus   Tropical Berries/Cherries</td></tr>
<tr><td colspan="5">Flowery   Earthy   Woody   Spicy   Other:</td></tr>
</table>

TASTE	Taste/Body: Light Medium Full Sharp Mellow/Smooth
	Acidity: Low Balanced High
	Tannins: Missing Pleasing Astringent
	Finish: Short Medium Long

My Rating: 1   2   3   4   5

Wine Tasting Notes

Vintage:	Varietal or Blend Name:	
Winery:	Region:	

	AROMA	
AROMA	Aroma/Bouquet Intensity: Low Medium High	
	Fruity: Green Ripe Fresh Cooked Dried Tree Fruit Citrus Tropical Berries/Cherries	
	Flowery Earthy Woody Spicy Other:	

TASTE	Taste/Body: Light Medium Full Sharp Mellow/Smooth
	Acidity: Low Balanced High
	Tannins: Missing Pleasing Astringent
	Finish: Short Medium Long
	My Rating: 1 2 3 4 5

Wine Tasting Notes

Vintage:	Varietal or Blend Name:	
Winery:	Region:	

	AROMA	
AROMA	Aroma/Bouquet Intensity: Low Medium High	
	Fruity: Green Ripe Fresh Cooked Dried Tree Fruit Citrus Tropical Berries/Cherries	
	Flowery Earthy Woody Spicy Other:	

TASTE	Taste/Body: Light Medium Full Sharp Mellow/Smooth
	Acidity: Low Balanced High
	Tannins: Missing Pleasing Astringent
	Finish: Short Medium Long
	My Rating: 1 2 3 4 5

Wine Tasting Notes

Vintage:	Varietal or Blend Name:	
Winery:	Region:	

A R O M A	Aroma/Bouquet Intensity: Low Medium High	
	Fruity: Green Ripe Fresh Cooked Dried	
	Tree Fruit Citrus Tropical Berries/Cherries	
	Flowery Earthy Woody Spicy Other:	
T A S T E	Taste/Body: Light Medium Full Sharp Mellow/Smooth	
	Acidity: Low Balanced High	
	Tannins: Missing Pleasing Astringent	
	Finish: Short Medium Long	
My Rating:	1 2 3 4 5	

Wine Tasting Notes

Vintage:	Varietal or Blend Name:	
Winery:	Region:	

A R O M A	Aroma/Bouquet Intensity: Low Medium High	
	Fruity: Green Ripe Fresh Cooked Dried	
	Tree Fruit Citrus Tropical Berries/Cherries	
	Flowery Earthy Woody Spicy Other:	
T A S T E	Taste/Body: Light Medium Full Sharp Mellow/Smooth	
	Acidity: Low Balanced High	
	Tannins: Missing Pleasing Astringent	
	Finish: Short Medium Long	
My Rating:	1 2 3 4 5	

Wine Tasting Notes

Vintage:	Varietal or Blend Name:
Winery:	Region:

AROMA	
	Aroma/Bouquet Intensity: Low Medium High
	Fruity: Green Ripe Fresh Cooked Dried Tree Fruit Citrus Tropical Berries/Cherries
	Flowery Earthy Woody Spicy Other:

TASTE	
	Taste/Body: Light Medium Full Sharp Mellow/Smooth
	Acidity: Low Balanced High
	Tannins: Missing Pleasing Astringent
	Finish: Short Medium Long
My Rating: 1 2 3 4 5	

Wine Tasting Notes

Vintage:	Varietal or Blend Name:
Winery:	Region:

AROMA	
	Aroma/Bouquet Intensity: Low Medium High
	Fruity: Green Ripe Fresh Cooked Dried Tree Fruit Citrus Tropical Berries/Cherries
	Flowery Earthy Woody Spicy Other:

TASTE	
	Taste/Body: Light Medium Full Sharp Mellow/Smooth
	Acidity: Low Balanced High
	Tannins: Missing Pleasing Astringent
	Finish: Short Medium Long
My Rating: 1 2 3 4 5	

Wine Tasting Notes

Vintage:	Varietal or Blend Name:				
Winery:		Region:			

AROMA	Aroma/Bouquet Intensity:	Low	Medium		High
	Fruity: Green Ripe Fresh Cooked Dried Tree Fruit Citrus Tropical Berries/Cherries				
	Flowery Earthy Woody Spicy Other:				
TASTE	Taste/Body: Light Medium Full Sharp Mellow/Smooth				
	Acidity: Low Balanced High				
	Tannins: Missing Pleasing Astringent				
	Finish: Short Medium Long				
My Rating:	1 2 3 4 5				

Wine Tasting Notes

Vintage:	Varietal or Blend Name:				
Winery:		Region:			

AROMA	Aroma/Bouquet Intensity:	Low	Medium		High
	Fruity: Green Ripe Fresh Cooked Dried Tree Fruit Citrus Tropical Berries/Cherries				
	Flowery Earthy Woody Spicy Other:				
TASTE	Taste/Body: Light Medium Full Sharp Mellow/Smooth				
	Acidity: Low Balanced High				
	Tannins: Missing Pleasing Astringent				
	Finish: Short Medium Long				
My Rating:	1 2 3 4 5				